The *GOLF Magazine*
Golfer's Handbook

By

Peter Morrice

and the Editors of *GOLF Magazine*

Photography by Sam Greenwood

THE LYONS PRESS
Guilford, Connecticut
An imprint of The Globe Pequot Press

Contents

The Lyons Press is an imprint of The Globe Pequot Press.

10 9 8 7 6 5 4 3 2 1

Printed in the United States of America

ISBN 1-59228-390-X

Library of Congress Cataloging-in-Publication Data is available on file.

1

Preswing

Next time you go to the driving range, take a look at the folks around you. Chances are, you'll be standing in the midst of middle-handicap America. Ask around and you'll find they're trying to fix their slice, get more distance, hit the ball higher, and so on. All noble intentions, but most golfers think they'll naturally groove a better swing simply by hitting ball after ball until their hands throb. In the end, all they get is tired.

Now compare this scene of panting, ball-beating middle handicappers to the practice area at a professional tour event. If you've never been to one, trust me when I tell you the pros hit balls about half as fast as amateurs do. And what are most of them focusing on? Preswing fundamentals. Things

Tour pros work long hours on perfecting their setup.

like alignment and ball position and posture. They know that how they set up either promotes or prevents the right positions during the swing. They also know it's a lot easier to monitor and change static positions than swing positions.

You may find it amazing that the world's best players work on simple things that many amateurs think they had figured out years ago, but it's true. Every day the pros go back to the basics, knowing these are the building blocks of the golf swing. Let that be a revelation to you.

Jack Nicklaus, in his instruction manual *Golf My Way* wrote, "I think it [the setup] is the single most important maneuver in golf. . . . If you set up correctly, there's a good chance you'll hit a reasonable shot, even if you make a mediocre swing. If you set up incorrectly, you'll hit a lousy shot even if you make the greatest swing in the world." Actually, you *need* to make a faulty swing if it starts from a faulty setup. In effect, by making errors at address you require in-swing errors to compensate for them.

So, put aside that feeling that you already know how to set up to a golf ball. If you'd like to play better, do what the pros do and perfect your address positions. It's the only logical place to start.

The Grip

If you're like most golfers, the last thing you want to hear is that you have to change your grip. Golf is a humbling game in which you're constantly trying to assert control yet often feel like you have none. Your grip is your one connection to the golf club, and whether it's good or bad, it's yours. You rely on it for a sense of control, and no golfer wants to give that up.

But before you dismiss the idea of changing your grip, answer this: Would you like to get rid of that slice of yours? How about hitting the ball another 20 yards? Ahhh, now I've got your attention. Fact is, how you grip the club at address in large part determines the position of the clubface at impact, which plays a major role in the direction of your shots. The grip also figures prominently in how much power you can produce during the swing. In short, if you care about how far and how straight you hit the ball, you need to care about your grip.

Hitting It Straight

The way you grip the club influences how the clubface rotates during the swing—from open to square to closed like a swinging door. And the position of the clubface at impact dictates how the ball will curve in the air. For example, if the clubface is angled to the right, or "open," when it contacts the ball, the ball will pick up left-to-right sidespin and curve to the right. If the clubface is angled to the left, or "closed," the ball will take on right-to-left sidespin and curve left. It's that simple: The squareness of the clubface when it meets the ball is the only factor that affects the curvature of the shot.

But how does the way you grip the club affect clubface position at impact? Consider this: Your hands are pulled into certain positions on the downswing by the centrifugal force of the swing, like they would be in a game of tug-of-war. Let's call these "natural positions." If the hands don't match these natural positions at address, the clubface will either open or close when the hands assume these positions on the downswing.

The natural position for your left hand is however it hangs at your side; this is how it will return to the ball at impact. The position of your right hand is a different story, as the right hand makes a striking, or spanking, action at impact. To promote this, your right palm should point to the target at address. If your hands start in these positions and your clubface is square to the target, your clubface will return square at impact without manipulation.

Power Is in Your Hands

How does the correct grip promote more power in your swing? Think about what happens to your wrists as you swing back and through: They hinge the club up going back, unhinge coming down, and

Your right palm should face the target at address.

then rehinge on the follow-through. Get a club and try it. This may seem like a natural and inconsequential action, but it is a major power generator in the golf swing.

As the wrists hinge going back, they create an angle between the left arm and the club, thereby introducing a second lever to the swing. (The first lever, a straight line from the left shoulder to the clubhead, is established at address.) As wrist hinge produces this second lever, the clubhead can travel through a much longer arc than it could in a single-lever motion. And a longer arc means more room

Proper wrist hinge promotes a full swing arc.

Handle With Care

Grip thickness is one equipment variable that receives little attention. While standard, off-the-rack grips are fine for many golfers, make sure your grips are right for you. The critical check is in the left hand. Take your normal left-hand grip and check that the tips of your middle two fingers are lightly touching your palm. If the fingertips are either not reaching the palm or digging into it, your grips are the wrong size, which can have a profound effect on how you move the club.

for the clubhead to accelerate on the downswing. Furthermore, as centrifugal force on the downswing unhinges the wrists, pulling the left arm and the club back into a straight line, the clubhead is flung into the ball with great force. That's the whipping action you see in good players.

Believe it or not, the grip is at the root of this wrist action. To understand this, get a club and place the grip diagonally across your left palm, running from your forefinger to your heel pad, and close your fingers around it. Now, with your hand at your side, try to cock the clubhead up in front of you simply by hinging your left wrist. Not easy, right? Now grip the club again, this time holding the handle across the base of your fingers, and try that same exercise. You'll find you can cock the clubhead up farther and with greater ease with the handle in your fingers.

This is precisely how the left wrist should hinge during the golf swing and the reason the handle

The popular Vardon, or overlapping grip.

must be held in the fingers of the left hand. Like-wise with the right hand, as the right wrist also must hinge. With the handle placed correctly and the hands in their natural positions on the club, the hands and arms can contribute significant power and also square the clubface at impact.

How to Find Your Best Grip

Let your left hand hang at your side. Your palm probably doesn't directly face your left leg; with most people, it's rotated slightly inward. To demon-strate this, lay a pencil loosely in your fingers and again let your hand hang. Is the pencil sticking straight out? It's likely pointing slightly to the right. This is the natural position of your left hand, a posi-tion it will seek out unless forced otherwise, so place your hand like this on the grip.

Generally speaking, the handle should run from the middle of your left forefinger to just under the heel pad of the hand. When you close your fingers around the grip, feel as if you're holding the handle against your palm with your fingers, the butt of the club sitting firmly under the heel pad. Then add the right hand, also setting the handle in the fingers. The visual here is that the right palm should face the target at address, matching the clubface, as it will make a palm-to-target striking action at impact.

As for how to join the hands, most instructors recommend the Vardon, or overlapping, grip, where the little finger of the right hand hooks around the left forefinger. For most golfers, this arrangement offers the best combination of control in the fingers and range of motion in the wrists.

BEST TIP: *The Impact Test*

Centrifugal force causes the joints of the left wrist, elbow, and shoulder to line up in a certain way at impact. An effective grip delivers a square clubface as this lining up occurs.

You can simulate this pulling force as follows: Grip a 5-iron in your left hand as you normally do and hold the club out in front of you with the toe straight up. Have a friend hook his fingers around the clubhead. Then slowly lean back, letting your body weight straighten out your left arm (see photo at right). This is how your joints will line up at impact. If your grip is good, your clubface will remain square, or toe-up, as you lean back. If the clubhead twists left or right, adjust your left-hand grip accordingly.

—Robert Baker, *GOLF Magazine*
Master Teaching Professional

Tension Control

There are all sorts of images out there for monitoring grip pressure. Sam Snead used to say to pretend you're holding a baby bird, while another image equates grip pressure to squeezing a tube of toothpaste. While these thoughts may be helpful, you alone have to determine how much pressure is right for your swing.

You should feel as though you're gripping as lightly as you can without losing control of the club during the swing. Due to the swing's high velocity, you need a secure hold with your fingers, but you don't want to create undue tension in your wrists and forearms. Setting the handle in your fingers, not your palms, will help keep the wrists and arms relaxed, as flexing the hand muscles sends tension up the arms.

Experiment on the practice tee with different levels of grip pressure. When you find one that seems right for you, rate it on a scale of 1 to 10 (1 being the lightest; 10 the tightest). If your ideal grip is a 5, for instance, make that one of your preswing checkpoints. You'll be amazed how much faster you can swing the club with a lighter grip.

> ### BEST TIP: The Pincher Drill
>
> Excessive pressure in the last three fingers of each hand causes the forearms to become rigid. To relieve this tension, make some pitch swings using a "pincher grip," with just the thumb and forefinger of each hand gripping the club and the other six fingers flared out. Notice how well you can control the club with such little grip pressure. Try to incorporate more "pinch pressure" into your normal grip.
>
> —Kip Puterbaugh, *GOLF Magazine*
> Top 100 Teacher

Aim and Alignment

Golf is a game of precision disguised as a walk in the park. Think about it: You stand on most tees and gaze out over a 40-yard-wide target, any part of which you'd be happy to play your next shot from. Then you hit into greens bigger than most backyards—and again, you'll take any shot that ends up on the putting surface. In fact, it seems the only time you have a specific target is when you're putting. And they call this a target sport?

They do, and it most certainly is. However, many golfers get lulled into complacency, even sheer sloppiness, by the apparent size of their targets. They set up to shots as if direction is of little concern, and then can't believe it when their ball sails into trouble. It's crazy: Golfers try so hard to get their swing right so they can hit the ball well, and when they do, it goes in the wrong direction because of careless aim and alignment.

Granted, there are legions of faults that cause shots to fly off-line, but poor aim and alignment are among the biggest culprits. And since they occur before the swing begins, they are the easiest to rectify. Unfortunately, some golfers find the aiming process mundane and therefore disregard it; others fail to appreciate the consequences. Whatever the reason, the golfer who neglects these preshot essentials is leaving his performance up to chance: A perfect swing is wasted if it isn't preceded by good aim and alignment.

A Game of Direction

First, let's get our definitions down. "Aim" refers to the position of the clubface relative to the target, while "alignment" refers to the position of the body relative to the target line—an imaginary line drawn from the ball to the target. It's useful to think of

"Aim" is the angle of the clubface relative to the target.

aiming and aligning as two different actions, because they affect shot direction in different ways.

Aiming sets the clubface at address, which often determines its position at impact and therefore the way the ball curves in the air. But ball flight is a function not only of curvature, but also of the shot's starting direction; this is where alignment enters the picture.

On full shots, the path of the swing primarily determines the ball's starting direction; the momentum of the clubhead propels the ball in whatever direction it's tracking on. This swing direction tends to

Swing path mainly determines a shot's starting direction.

follow the alignment of the body lines—imaginary lines across the feet, knees, hips, and shoulders. Although the body lines tend to line up with one another, the shoulders are the key, since the arms hang directly from the shoulder sockets. So, instead of checking the squareness of your stance to assess alignment, as most golfers do, have a friend hold a club across your shoulders to see where they're pointed; they have the biggest impact on swing path.

I have already touched upon clubface aim and how the grip plays a leading role in the rotation of the clubface during the swing. But the positioning of the clubface at address drives the entire aiming process. If you watch the pros, you'll see they aim the clubface first, then step into their stance and align their body. This order is critical: At address you have a better view of the clubface then you do your various body lines and can therefore aim the face with greater accuracy. Then, a square clubface can serve as a valuable reference point when you align your body.

How to Aim and Align

Should all golfers employ the same aim and alignment? In a perfect world, they would. If the clubface is perfectly square at impact and the clubhead is moving directly along the target line, the result is a shot that flies straight to the target. And straight shots should be preceded by square aim and alignment. However, golfers know such shots are few and far between.

More likely, you get into the habit of aiming and aligning a certain way as a reaction to your typical ball flight. For example, if you slice, you may start aligning to the left to make room for your left-to-right curve. The opposite goes for the golfer who tends to hook. But these are individual variations we cannot cover here, so let's establish a method for setting a square clubface and square alignment. You can vary from the model as necessary.

Starting from behind the ball, pick an intermediate target—an old divot hole, a patch of discolored grass—a few feet in front of the ball and directly on your target line. Walk to the side of the ball and set the clubhead behind it, positioning the leading edge (bottom) of the clubface perpendicular to your target line. This is where that intermediate target becomes helpful. It's much easier to square your clubface to a spot a few feet away than to a target a couple of hundred yards away.

Using the square clubface as a guide, position your feet, setting your stance line perpendicular to

First, square your clubface to your intermediate target.

Then, align your body parallel to the target line.

the clubface, which is also parallel to the target line. Check to see that imaginary lines across your knees, hips, and shoulders are all parallel to your stance. If they are, you have a square clubface and square alignment to match.

BEST TIP: Use an Aiming Station

Proper aim and alignment come from good habits. You have to learn to establish your target line and use it to aim your club and align your body.

To d o this, set up an aiming station the next time you go to the practice range. Lay down a 12- to 15-foot piece of rope to represent the line you want the shot to start on, then place a club on the ground in front of your toes and parallel to the rope. Lining up your feet with this club will effectively square your stance.

Hit some balls from this setup, first setting the leading edge of the clubface perpendicular to the rope, then setting your body lines parallel to the club on the ground. Getting into the habit of squaring the clubface and then matching your body will serve you well on the course.

—Jim Flick, *GOLF Magazine*
Master Teaching Professional

Ball Position and Stance

Of all the preswing elements, stance and ball position are probably the most instinctual. Ball position relies heavily on innate eye–hand coordination. Plus, you get direct feedback: If you're hitting behind the ball, it's too far forward; if you're hitting the top of it, it's too far back. Even rank beginners figure that out. And your stance is simply a way of arranging your feet to maintain balance during the swing, which you do naturally to support any motion.

The downside to these elements becoming second nature so quickly is that golfers tend to forget about them. As they gain more knowledge of the mechanics of the swing, they have "bigger fish to fry" than these elementary setup positions. Such thinking is a grave error, for although ball position and stance may not be exciting, they have a tremendous impact on performance. And they, too, can slip off track.

Take ball position. It's one of the first things Tour pros check when their ball-striking starts to slide. If this surprises you, consider why it's important in the first place. In order to fully benefit from the power and precision you work to create in your golf swing, you must hit the ball flush. To do this, you have to make contact with the ball at precisely the right point during the swing—or else your effort is wasted.

So where is this right point? With the driver, it's just after the clubhead has passed the low point in its arc and started to ascend. For all other shots, contact should come just before the clubhead reaches the low point. Remember, nothing ensures solid contact better than proper ball position.

Where to Play the Ball

Although many great players, including Jack Nicklaus, have been successful playing the ball in the same position for all shots, it's generally accepted

Play the driver off the left heel for a square hit.

Center the ball for the wedge for a descending blow.

today that the ball should move progressively farther back in the stance as the clubs get shorter.

First, understand that the swing will tend to bottom out directly below the swing center, or the sternum. The key to solid ball-striking is having the ball positioned so that you create the right sternum-to-ball relationship at impact—sternum behind the ball for the driver, about over the ball for a 5-iron, and slightly in front of the ball for a wedge.

If the driver is played off the left heel, as most teachers recommend, the 5-iron should be two to three inches behind that, and the wedge in about the middle of the stance. Why such big changes? With the longer clubs, the golfer moves aggressively toward the target on the downswing, which moves the swing arc forward and requires a forward ball position. With the shorter clubs, there's little lateral body thrust toward the target and therefore the ball should be played below the sternum to create the proper impact.

Customize Your Ball Position

You can easily determine your optimum ball position with each club based on your own individual swing. Grab your driver, 5-iron, and pitching wedge and find any flat grassy area. Starting with the wedge, make some normal practice swings, noting where the clubhead cuts through the grass. Do the same with your 5-iron, then your driver, marking their respective touchdown points with tees.

The location of the tees will tell you where you should position the ball for each club. Keep in mind, the exact ball position should be slightly behind the touchdown points for the irons, as you want to make ball-first contact. For the driver, position the ball slightly in front of the touchdown spot to promote a slight upswing hit. With a little experimentation, you'll identify the optimum ball position for the various clubs; then it's just a matter of keeping tabs on it from shot to shot and round to round.

BEST TIP: Distance from the Ball

Golfers often ask me how far they should stand from the ball. To answer them, I refer to a composite computer model that Dr. Ralph Mann and I generated from a biomechanical study using 54 PGA Tour pros. With the driver, the pros we tested addressed the ball with their left toe approximately 32 inches from the ball. Shorter golfers may want to increase that to 33 inches, taller players to 31. For a 5-iron, the pros stood 23 to 25 inches away; with a 9-iron, 19 to 21 inches. So, the next time you go to practice, slip a yardstick in your bag and see how you measure up.

—Fred Griffin, *GOLF Magazine* Top 100 Teacher

Good Standing

We've touched on the stance already, but let's take a more in-depth look at the basic rules. There are really two areas to consider when you position your feet: how wide apart to set them and how to angle them in relation to the target line.

Your stance should never be wider than it has to be for stability, as a wide stance restricts the natural motion of the hips and legs. In general, as the clubs become shorter, your stance should become narrower, your narrowest stance coming with the wedges. This is because the shorter clubs produce a steeper swinging motion and limited weight transfer and therefore don't require a wide stance for balance. The faster, more powerful swings made with the longer clubs produce weight transfer and rely on a wider stance for stability.

So how wide is right? Picture vertical lines drawn down from your shoulders. With a wedge, the outer edges of your feet should line up with these vertical lines; with a 5-iron, the middle of your feet should be on the lines; and with the driver, your insteps should correspond with the lines. Flexible players can spread their feet a bit more, but keep in mind, the more you widen your stance, the more you restrict body coil.

With a wedge, set the outsides of your feet at shoulder width.

Angling the feet at address also has a major influence on how the body works during the swing. Assuming the stance is square to the target, flaring either foot outward affects the body's turning capacity. If you flare out the right foot, the hips and therefore the shoulders turn more easily away from the target. Turn out the left foot and you facilitate

With a driver, set your insteps at shoulder width.

body turn toward the target on the downswing. Try these variations; you'll feel the difference.

Many teachers recommend a square right foot, set at a right angle to the target line, and a slightly flared left foot, opened roughly 20 degrees toward the target. Squaring the right foot limits the hip turn going back, providing resistance as the torso

A square right foot creates a tight backswing coil.

turns and letting the body coil like a spring. Flaring the left foot presets a quick uncoiling of the lower body on the downswing, a powerful move all golfers should strive for.

BEST TIP: A Guide for Wide

Your stance should never be wider than your normal walking stride. Most golfers err on the wide side, as they feel more powerful. Ironically, a wide stance actually reduces power by restricting body turn.

Here's how to establish your ideal stance width: Take a normal step forward with your left foot and stop. Spin 90 degrees to your right, keeping your toes in place. That's how wide you should stand with the driver. For each successive club, narrow your stance a half inch, which puts your feet five to six inches closer together for the short irons.

—John Redman, *GOLF Magazine*
Top 100 Teacher

Posture

Good posture, whether it be at the dinner table or walking down the street, makes a person look alert and confident. Poor posture, on the other hand, suggests sloppiness and fatigue and makes a person seem careless and decidedly less athletic.

In life, such generalizations may be unfair, but when it comes to golf, they do hold some truth. Fact is, the better your posture at address, the better your chance of making a powerful, consistent golf swing. This is not to suggest that your back has to be ramrod-straight, with your chin jutting high in the air; rather you should find a balance between textbook-perfect posture and posture that is comfortable for you.

Physics and kinesiology tell us there are ideal angles at which the body moves fastest and most efficiently. But when a golfer cannot easily create these angles at address or sustain them during the swing, he must make adjustments to his setup or else risk in-swing compensations. For example, a person with rounded shoulders should naturally slump over more than a person who has perfect posture. Point is, strained positions create tension, and tension is the number-one killer of golf swings.

It's a Balancing Act

One of the irksome things about this game is that the golf ball lies on the ground and the golfer stands almost upright. Immediately you're faced with a dilemma: how to get the clubhead down to the ball. There are two primary ways to lower yourself toward the ball: Tilt the torso forward (upper body) and flex the knees (lower body). Sounds easy enough, until you learn that effective posture is a delicate balance of the two.

For starters, the upper body should pitch forward from the hip sockets while the knees assume a

To set your posture, first tilt forward from the hips.

slight or "athletic" flex, like those of a tennis player awaiting a serve. The order in which you introduce these angles is critical: You must tilt the upper body first, which sets your weight forward, then you flex your knees just enough to redistribute the weight toward the middle of the feet. If you start with the knees, you'll tend to bend them too much and then

After you've pitched forward, add a slight flex to the knees.

set the upper body too upright, the most common posture fault among amateurs.

Once you assume your posture, you should feel balanced and stable, as if you could react in any direction without losing your footing. Golf is unlike many other sports in that you're not physically reacting to an opponent's moves; but in the case of address posture, try nevertheless to create a "ready" or "anticipatory" position, as if some action were coming your way.

BEST TIP: Get Vertically Aligned

The body posture to strive for at address is called "vertical alignment." This is a fancy way of saying you want your upper body balanced over your lower body. More specifically, you achieve this position if a straight line extending downward from the back of your shoulders (viewed from the side) would pass through your kneecaps and into the balls of your feet. Have a friend hang a club from the back of either shoulder to see how you line up at address.

—Rick McCord, *GOLF Magazine* Top 100 Teacher

A Second Tilt

Besides tilting toward the ball, your upper body should also tilt a few degrees away from the target at address. This slight lean to the right presets the coiling action of the upper body and weight trans-

Good Advice Gone Bad

Beginning golfers are constantly being told to keep their head down, because they tend to look up prematurely to see the shot. As a result of these constant reminders, many golfers become "ball bound," meaning they fixate on the ball at address. When this happens, the head invariably droops down, burying the chin in the chest. Then, when the shoulders try to turn on the backswing, the chin gets in the way and thereby cuts off the coiling action and shortens the swing. To prevent this, remind yourself at address to keep your head up and look at the ball through the bottoms of your eyes.

fer to the right leg on the backswing. The good news is, this tilt occurs naturally—if you let it.

Here's what happens: When a right-handed golfer grips a club, he places his right hand below his left on the handle, by about four inches. This position drops the right shoulder lower than the left and, since the shoulders are connected to the spine, tilts the spine slightly to the right. From there, the body will "load" onto the right side as the backswing is completed, setting up a powerful return to the ball.

There's more. When your spine tilts to the right, your head has little choice but to go with it. And that's a beneficial position as well, as your head needs to be behind the ball through impact to maximize the power and leverage of the swing.

Placing your right hand below your left on the grip tilts your spine away from the target.

Preshot Routine

Now that we've discussed the preswing compo-nents, we need to consider a system for putting them into place before every swing. This may

Is Your "K" Okay?

One of the most enduring images in golf instruction is the reverse "K" address position. It's created by the slight tilting of the spine away from the target. To see it, take your address facing a full-length mirror.

Draw an imaginary line from your left foot to your left shoulder; it should be fairly straight and tilt slightly away from the target. Then envision a similar line along your right side. It should run from your right shoulder to your waist, then kink and go down your right leg. Together these two lines should resemble the letter "K" turned backward. Check this position often, as it promotes many correct moves in the golf swing.

sound like a lot to keep track of, but the good news is human beings are creatures of habit: We thrive on the familiarity that habit brings. The trick is to make sure you form the right habits, which then serve as a barrier to keep the wrong ones out.

What you need is a sensible method for organizing the various elements of the setup. The best way to do this is to establish a preshot routine, a series of simple preparation tasks designed to get you physically and mentally ready to execute the shot at hand. As you think about making a preshot routine part of your game, remember that the better your setup, the better your odds of consistently making an effective golf swing. Address positions are literally the foundation of the swing. Get them right and you have something reliable on which to build.

Why All the Fuss?

The purpose of the preshot routine is twofold. First, it provides a logical framework for organizing the setup components; and second, it creates a consistent approach from one shot to the next. A good preshot routine ensures that you give due diligence to the setup and then sends you into the swing feeling confident and relaxed, knowing you've done everything possible to prepare yourself. This way you can ask your body to execute a golf swing and reasonably expect it to respond.

For starters, understand that in the moments preceding every shot, your mind and body will be engaged in some form of activity. If you use that time well, meaning you establish your setup and promote relaxation, you're putting yourself in position to perform well. If you use that time unwisely, thinking about too many things or just fidgeting over the ball, your performance is a crapshoot. The first step to consistent performance is consistent preparation.

Next time you watch the pros on television, notice how they all perform their own preshot routine. Some look simple; others seem elaborate and tedious. But the common denominator is they repeat their routine before every shot they play. They know that golf is a complicated game, and the more you can standardize it from shot to shot, the more you simplify it. So stop reinventing the wheel every time you step up to your ball. Start with an effective preshot routine and your performance and confidence level will soar.

A Few Preshot Guidelines

It's true that every preshot routine has its own personality, but that's not to say they don't have common components. Every routine should start with an assessment of the target area and should end with a relaxation check just before the start of the swing. In between, the various setup elements should be established, and extraneous thoughts and actions should be kept to an absolute minimum.

The best starting place for any shot is directly behind the ball, where you can clearly view the target area and envision the ball flight in your mind. This signals the start of your preshot routine, indicating it's time to clear your mind of any negative thoughts and to focus on creating a perfect setup. The theme from start to finish should be simplicity and structure. In the end, your routine should not be mentally taxing and should be easy to repeat time and time again.

Get a Good View

Standing a few paces behind the ball, first establish your ultimate target. This may not be the middle of the fairway or the flag, due to the proximity of hazards or the ideal angle for your next shot. For instance, if you're a short hitter playing a hole that doglegs to the left 250 yards out, you may want to play to the right side off the tee to set up a clear approach. Whatever the case, pick a target that's realistic for you, always considering your next play.

Keep in mind, your target line probably isn't the line you want to start your shot on. If you tend to curve the ball either left or right, you need to borrow some room to allow for that curve—perhaps 10 to 20 yards. Once you establish a starting line for the shot, pick an intermediate target, as described earlier, directly on that line and a few feet in front of your ball. You'll use this intermediate spot at address to establish precise aim and alignment.

Some players like to take their grip while standing behind the ball, which is fine. Since we've already discussed how to arrange your hands, just note that you must make sure the clubface is square once your grip is complete. To do this, raise the clubhead up to waist level after you've taken your grip: The clubface is square if the leading edge,

From behind the ball, pick an intermediate target directly on your starting line.

or bottom, of the face is perpendicular to the ground. Now you're ready to step into the shot.

Step to the Side

If you wish to take a practice swing, do so as soon as you walk to the side of the ball. Practice swings can be useful in relieving tension or rehearsing a particular swing, but eliminate them if you feel they interrupt the flow of the preshot routine or offer little preparation value. Players who lack patience or find themselves rushing through the preshot process should consider skipping the practice swing and focusing on the essential preshot elements, such as aim and alignment. It may be reassuring to rehearse your swing, but to do so in lieu of a proper setup is only hurting your chances.

Once you're ready to step up to the ball, your first objective should be to square the clubface to your starting line. Locate your intermediate target, then tilt your upper body forward to lower the clubhead to the ball. Set the leading edge of the clubface behind the ball and perpendicular to your starting line. If you haven't already completed your grip, now's the time to do it—left hand first, then

Square your clubface before taking your stance.

right. Make sure the clubface is square to your starting line when your grip is complete.

Using the clubface as a guide, set your feet parallel to your intended starting line. To do this, it might help to picture your setup as a T square, with your clubface flush to the ruler's edge and the tips of your shoes up against either end of the "T." Although your other body lines tend to follow the alignment of your feet, it's a good idea to run your eyes from your toes to your shoulders, making sure these lines are parallel to one another.

At this point, your body weight should be favoring your toes, as you've tilted your upper body forward to sole the clubhead. To counter this, flex your knees slightly to redistribute the weight toward the middle of each foot. Remember, keep your knee bend to a minimum. Your lower body should feel ready to support the momentum of the swing but not be in a strained or aggressive pose.

One last thing before you start your swing: Check your relaxation level. Tension at address leads to a fast takeaway and limited range of motion. The two most popular ways to curb tension are waggling the clubhead and taking deep breaths. The waggle keeps your hands and arms supple so they can create a smooth start to the swing, while deep breathing can relieve muscle tension throughout your body. Although it's a good idea to monitor your breathing throughout the preshot process, the most important time is just before you start the club back. Feel the breathing down in your diaphragm, not just in your upper chest. The relaxation you create will really pay off.

It's a Golfer's Best Friend

Golf at times seems a cruel and lonely game. But with an effective preshot routine on your side, you can create a sense of familiarity and reassurance be-

A Sample Preshot Routine

Behind the ball:

1. Pick your target and starting line for the shot.
2. Select an intermediate target in front of the ball.
3. Complete your grip.

Beside the ball:

4. Make a practice swing to rehearse the feel.
5. Using the intermediate target, square the club-face.
6. Using the square club-face, align your body.
7. Complete your posture.
8. Relaxation check: waggle or deep breath.

fore every swing you make. It's a lot easier to be relaxed over the ball knowing you've achieved the correct setup positions and done all you can to ready your mind and body.

Furthermore, a reliable preshot routine will do wonders for your performance under pressure. When a stressful situation arises, such as teeing off in front of a crowd or playing sudden death in a match, most golfers either speed up or try to carefully control every step of the process. The speedsters wind up swinging before they've adequately prepared their mind or body, while the deliberate types only add to the gravity of the moment. The key in pressure situations is using the same routine you've grooved when the pressure wasn't on; that's the best way to counter the anxiety you feel.

BEST TIP: *Perform at Peak Concentration*

The amount of time it takes to perform the preshot routine is critical yet often overlooked. Each golfer has his own capacity to concentrate, and for every shot he faces, there's one moment in time when his concentration is at its peak. Your objective should be to reach that peak and act then.

Over the years, I've timed about 50 PGA Tour players to see how long they take to hit a shot. Three-quarters of them took between 18 and 22 seconds from the moment they clicked "on" their concentration to contact with the ball. Each had his own preshot routine, which never varied from shot to shot, and each took a consistent amount of time to hit the ball.

Experiment with preshot routines of varying lengths on the practice range and have a friend time each one with a stopwatch. Over time, your performance and patience level will tell you if you need a concise or detailed approach. Once you know, create a preshot routine to fit your concentration capacity and then use it before every swing you make.

—Dr. Richard Coop, *GOLF Magazine*
Mental Game Consultant

2

The Swing

Think of the golf swing like a game of dominoes: Set it up, get it started, and the rest takes care of itself. Okay, it's not quite that simple, but the swing *is* a natural chain of events—and doesn't have to be as complicated as many amateurs make it. With all the mental and physical factors you can try to control, it's no wonder the average player often seems frustrated and confused. He is, much of the time, simply overwhelmed.

But it doesn't have to be that way. First of all, understand that the outcome of your shots is largely determined by decisions you make before you step up to the ball, such as club selection, shot selection, and target orientation. If any of these factors are off, your outcome will suffer despite how well you execute your swing. It's during the preswing period that the golfer has to be a thinker.

After these preliminary decisions, your focus becomes the setup, which we've established as a major factor in performance. How major? Look at it this way: You take your setup—a structured, step-by-step procedure—and all that's left is making the swing itself, which should be an instinctive, flowing action. This is where athleticism must take over.

Remember, almost all of the thinking you do on a given shot should be completed before you take the club back. The angles and positions we are about to discuss should be grooved on the practice tee, not on the golf course. Mechanical thoughts cause tension, and tension is your swing's biggest enemy. So, consider yourself forewarned: Think while you practice and before you execute. Once you start your swing, rely as much as possible on your athletic instincts.

Starting Back

Put simply, the takeaway sets the shape and pace of the golf swing. A swing that starts off smoothly, the arms and body moving in sync, has a good chance of producing favorable results. One that starts quickly or out of sequence demands in-swing compensations, which are unreliable at best.

There are several keys to a good takeaway. First of all, it should not start from a still position, one good reason to waggle the club at address, as described earlier. Another effective preswing motion is the forward press, whereby the golfer pushes his hands slightly toward the target immediately before starting the club back. In this case, the takeaway is essentially a rebound of the forward press.

Starting back, the hands, arms, and shoulders should move the club away together. This is called a "one-piece takeaway." Such connection at the start is critical to creating the right path and shape for the swing. You should feel like the left shoulder is pushing the club back, without any conscious twisting or hinging of the hands or wrists.

When the clubhead reaches hip high, there are three important positions to check. First, the shaft should be parallel to the target line, the butt end of the grip pointing just left of the target. Second, there should only be a slight hinge in the left wrist,

Tailor Your Waggle

Aside from kick-starting the swing, the waggle can also serve as a rehearsal of your takeaway. Consider this: Most golfers either lift the club abruptly on the takeaway or else drag it back with tense arms and stiff wrists. If you have either problem, design a waggle to prevent it. Use a wide, one-piece waggle to head off an abrupt start, or a loose, wristy waggle to avoid a rigid, mechanical takeaway. Take advantage of your rehearsal.

At hip high, the shaft should be parallel to the target line.

During the takeaway, the wrists should hinge only slightly.

as this initial move is a wide, sweeping motion. And third, the toe of the clubhead should be turned upward, as the forearms naturally start to rotate. With the clubhead hip high, the leading edge of the clubface should match the forward tilt of your spine. Get these positions right and you've created a wide extension and the proper path for your golf swing.

The only other factor to consider on the takeaway is tempo. This needs to be the slowest part of your swing. If the takeaway is fast or abrupt, the swing will follow suit; likewise, if you start with a smooth, wide extension, you're likely to maintain good rhythm and width throughout your swing. So remember, think slow at the start: The swing is plenty long enough to produce acceleration without any quick bursts of speed in the early going.

BEST TIP: Get a Head Start

To groove a wide, smooth extension away from the ball, hit some practice shots starting from a fully extended postimpact position. (Set up as usual, then move the clubhead out a few feet toward the target, fully extending your arms as you do after impact.) From there, just take your normal backswing. Starting from a full extension (see photo at right) promotes a wide, smooth move going back.

—Dick Tiddy, *GOLF Magazine* Top 100 Teacher

To the Top

Once the clubhead reaches hip high, the majority of the body weight should already be on the right instep. This weight transfer occurs as a natural result of the arms and shoulders extending the clubhead away from the ball. If your weight is still centered at this point, chances are you've made an abrupt takeaway by lifting the club with your hands and cocking your wrists.

From the hip-high position, the wrists will start to hinge the club upward, as long as they are free of excess tension. In fact, by the time the hands are opposite the right ear, the wrists should have cocked the club into a 90-degree angle with the left arm, creating a distinct second lever in the swing. This second lever not only allows the clubhead to swing through a much longer arc in the backswing, but also sets up a powerful release of energy on the downswing. Wrist cock is one of the hallmarks of a powerful swing.

Just Plane Talk

Swing plane is a daunting topic to many golfers, so let's simplify it. The plane of the golf swing is established by the angle of the shaft to the ground at address (looking down the target line). As a general rule, a swing is called "on plane" if the club stays parallel to this address angle throughout the swing. Longer clubs create a flatter plane, as the golfer stands farther from the ball to accommodate the longer shafts, while shorter clubs put the golfer closer to the ball and therefore produce a more upright swing plane. But while the shaft angle at ad-

Going back, the wrists should hinge the club into a 90-degree angle with the left arm.

dress varies from club to club, the shaft should stay roughly parallel to this starting angle throughout the swing—and that goes for every club in the bag.

To further understand the concept of swinging on plane, picture your target line extending infinitely both toward and away from the target. At address, the shaft points directly at this line. As the club starts back, it sweeps inside and starts to elevate, but the shaft still points directly at the extended target line. As the swing progresses and the wrists hinge, the club turns upside down. Now the butt end of the club points to the extended target line. In fact, either the clubhead end or the butt end, whichever is closer to the ground, should point to this extended line throughout the entire swing.

Although the plane of the swing actually should get slightly flatter coming down than it was going back—as the forward thrust of the lower body on the downswing pulls the club into a flatter position—for simplicity's sake, stick to the extended target line image to check your swing plane.

Load Before You Fire

The purpose of the backswing is to position the club and coil the body in such a way that the downswing

At halfway back, the grip end should point to the ball.

is a simple reversal of events. As I've said, the farther along you get, the harder it is to assert control
over the swing; by the time the downswing begins,
if not sooner, you have to be on automatic pilot.

After the wrists have fully hinged, the hips and
shoulders continue to turn to complete the backswing. It's important to remember that once the
shoulders stop turning, the arms should stop
swinging back. If they don't, the body will likely
start down before the arms are ready, throwing the
swing out of sync. Ideally, the shoulders turn 90 degrees and the hips 45 degrees from their starting
positions to the top of the backswing. This relationship between the upper body and lower body coils
the torso like a spring, setting up a powerful uncoiling on the downswing.

Now let's discuss the role of the lower body in
the backswing. Most teachers view the lower body
as the support base for the actions of the upper
body. As such, the legs do not initiate any backswing action. In fact, the lower body should resist
the turning of the upper body to create the spring-
like effect that will power the downswing. In short,
the legs should simply maintain their flex and react
to the coiling of the torso, the right leg serving as
the axis over which the upper body rotates.

If the lower body stays passive, the torso coils like a spring.

> ## BEST TIP: Light Up Your Line
>
> Here's a good visual for checking your swing plane. Line up two clubs on the ground, one on either side of the ball, to represent your target line. Then tape two flashlights together end to end, so the beams shine in opposite directions. Grip the flashlights like a club and take your setup, shining one beam on the ball. Take some slow-motion half-swings: If your swing is perfectly on-plane, the beam from one flashlight, then the other should shine on the clubs going back. Coming down, again one beam, then the other should track along the clubs.
>
> —Rick Grayson, *GOLF Magazine*
> Top 100 Teacher

Checkpoints at the Top

The top of the backswing offers one last chance to check yourself before "letting it go." Not that you should have swing thoughts at this point; your thinking should be geared toward the setup and maybe the very early part of the swing. But, when practicing, it is useful to swing to the top and assess what your swing looks and feels like. The downswing happens too fast to include reliable compensations for bad positions at the top.

At the top, the upper body should feel fully coiled, with the left shoulder turned under the chin. The left arm should be fairly straight, although not stiff, and the back of the left hand should be in a straight line with the left forearm, neither cupped nor bowed. Ideally, the club should be parallel to your target line and in a fully horizontal position. A square clubface at the top, assuming you've swung it all the way back, puts the leading edge at the same angle as your left forearm—roughly 45 degrees to the ground.

The lower body should feel stable and ready to start moving toward the target. Most of the body weight should be distributed between the right instep and heel, never to the outside of the right foot, and the left knee should be kicked in slightly.

Most golfers keep their left heel planted throughout the backswing, although inflexible players may consider letting the momentum of the backswing pull it an inch or two off the ground to allow for a fuller swing. Nevertheless, even if the heel is lifted, the left toe should still be gripping the ground, as the body must be in position to shift left and drive toward the target.

For a full coil, feel your left shoulder turn under your chin.

Stay in Those Angles

An effective backswing winds the body up and sets the club in a position at the top from which it is easy to simply reverse directions and deliver the club forcefully to the ball. The key word here is "simply," as many golfers make moves on the backswing that have to be undone on the down-swing if the clubhead is to accurately return to the ball.

The most important area when it comes to keeping your swing simple is posture. In short, you have to maintain the same body posture from address through impact in order to achieve any degree of ball-striking consistency. If your posture changes going back, meaning you raise up or shrink down, you have to make the exact reversal of that move on the downswing to strike the ball solidly.

As noted earlier, posture is a combination of forward tilt from the hips and flex in the knees. Although these critical body angles vary from player to player, based on individual physique, once they're established at address, they must remain fixed through contact with the ball. This can be a challenging endeavor, especially for less flexible players, since the address position can feel awkward even before the body starts coiling.

To add to the difficulty, the coiling action of the backswing jeopardizes these angles in two ways. First, it's easier to turn your shoulders from a more upright position, which encourages you to raise up as the shoulders near their rotational limit. Second, as weight transfers to your back foot, it's easy to let it drift to the outside of the foot, which often causes

---

BEST TIP: *Feel a Good Coil*

Coil is created when you wind the upper body against the resistance of the lower body. To feel this, sit on a bench or chair and lean forward 30 degrees. Grip a club and start to swing back, turning your left shoulder toward your chin. Since you can't turn your hips at all while sitting, you'll feel the large muscles of your back start to stretch almost immediately. Try to reproduce this coiled feeling in your golf swing.

—Carl Lohren, *GOLF Magazine* Top 100 Teacher

---

the back knee to straighten. These tendencies make it all the more important to be aware of maintaining your posture through impact.

One good way to make sure you're staying in posture is to swing in front of a full-length mirror with a mark or piece of tape indicating your head level at address. Swing back and through several times, looking up to check that your head doesn't move above or below its starting position until it turns up on the follow-through.

The Transition

We've said that the takeaway sets the overall shape and pace of the swing, but the transition from backswing to downswing has the most direct effect on the shape and pace of the down-swing. In other words, the way the golfer changes direction at the top in large part determines his position at impact, which is the only position that dictates where the ball goes.

The keys to a good transition are proper sequence of motion and smooth tempo. Most teachers hold that the downswing should occur from the ground up, starting with a weight transfer or lateral "bump" back to the front foot. From there, the body should start un-

Don't Pause

Players who tend to rush the club back down to the ball are often told to pause at the top. This is dangerous advice for two reasons. First, the swing should always be thought of as one flowing motion: Any conscious starting or stopping disrupts its natural rhythm. Second, a pause at the top reduces the resistance between the upper and lower body, promoting a downswing in which the entire body unwinds together. The result is a lack of leverage on the downswing and a dramatic loss of power.

winding, lower body leading and pulling the upper body, until the club is pulled through by the momentum of this uncoiling action. There need be no conscious flipping of the hands through the hitting area: If the body is allowed to unwind in sequence, centrifugal force will properly position the hands and arms at impact.

If the downswing is simply a reversal of the backswing, it must begin with a return of the weight to the front foot. In fact, the lower body actually should

The downswing starts with a lateral "bump" back to the front foot.

start toward the target a split second before the upper body finishes turning back. This stretches the muscles involved in the coil even more and gives the appearance that the clubhead lags behind in the downswing sequence. The immortal Bobby Jones described this action in his book *Golf Is My Game* as follows, "The all-important feel which I experience as the swing changes direction is one of leaving the clubhead at the top of the swing."

> ### BEST TIP: *Uncoil from the Ground Up*
>
> Grip a three-foot-long piece of rope as if it were a golf club and swing it back, letting it flip over your right shoulder. From there, swing the rope down and through, letting the lower body lead the uncoiling action, pulling the rope taut and making the tip trail through the hitting area. This drill proves that the downswing is a pulling motion, as the lower body must lead the upper body for the tip of the rope to whip through last.
>
> —Martin Hall, *GOLF Magazine*
> Master Teaching Professional

Watch Your Speed

Just like the first move away from the ball, the transition from backswing to downswing should be smooth and unhurried. In fact, a graceful transition is one of the most aesthetically pleasing parts of the golf swing.

Think of the great players you like to watch. I'll bet they include such smooth swingers as Fred Couples, Ernie Els, and Steve Elkington. These players seem to have effortless power—no sudden bursts of speed, yet an aggressive whip into the ball. Much of this graceful power comes from a smooth transition, which allows them to gradually accelerate the club through impact. The simple truth is that the more you rush the swing from the top, the less speed you'll have at impact. Your swing can only have one fast point—save it for when it counts.

If you think smooth tempo is an intangible quality and either you have it or you don't, you're half right. The world's top golfers are gifted athletes with a natural sense of rhythm and timing, but that doesn't mean you can't improve your own speed control. If you can calm the instinct to "hit from the top" and trust that gradual acceleration will yield maximum swing speed, you'll groove a more powerful, more consistent golf swing.

How to Find "The Slot"

If, as we've said, an effective downswing should simply undo the positions achieved on the backswing, this means the arms, which travel in and up going back, must reverse that motion so that they move down and out—in that order. Unfortunately, most golfers don't let the club drop down before they swing it out to the ball. As we'll see later, the "over-the-top" downswing that results is one of the most prevalent faults in the game.

The fall of the arms at the start of the downswing is one of the marks of an accomplished player. The good news is, it's a move that happens naturally if you follow the correct sequence of motion from the top. In other words, you don't have to consciously pull your arms down; a proper transition will drop them into position.

Let me explain. From a fully wound position at the top, your first move down—a lateral shift back to your front foot—will cause your arms to drop downward toward your right side. As the uncoiling of the body begins, the left shoulder pulls away from the chin, which also pulls the arms downward. Again, this dropping action is merely a response to the body's move toward the target, not a conscious action.

If the arms remain passive at the start of the downswing, they will fall into a position called "the slot," with the right elbow tucked close to the right side, the wrists still fully hinged, and the butt of the club pointing to the ball. This position sets the stage for a powerful delivery from inside the target line. Virtually all good ballstrikers, despite any idiosyncrasies on the backswing,

Don't Get Down

The idea that you have to hit down on the ball is one of the biggest misconceptions in the game. Truth is, the club should move at about a 90-degree angle to the spine on the downswing. The up-and-down appearance of the swing is created by the forward tilt of the spine at address. The golf swing is very much like a baseball swing; it just starts from a more bent-over position.

If the arms stay passive at the start of the downswing, the club drops into "the slot."

drop the club into the slot. Stay relaxed and let your swing unwind and you can, too.

Through Impact

Once you get into the downswing, you've reached the point of no return. You simply cannot manipulate the swing from this point forward with any degree of consistency. You've had your chances to affect the fate of the shot at hand, from club selection to setup positions to even a simple thought at the change of direction. Now the swing is on its own. The flight of the ball will tell you how well you've done.

This is not to suggest that you shouldn't be sensing anything through impact, only that trying to time specific positions when the club should be freewheeling into the ball is unwise and unreliable. You can, and should, feel certain sensations as the body uncoils, but they are "flowing" sensations that occur throughout the downswing. Among them are the transition of weight to the front foot and the pulling of the torso and arms by the lower body. Let's try to isolate these feelings and thereby create a sensory framework for the downswing. You may not be able to "save the swing" at this point, but you can sense how it's going.

Shift, Then Turn

While the lower body plays only a supporting role on the backswing, it takes center stage at the change of direction. After the initial forward shift of the lower body, the hips should start to rotate aggressively toward the target. This rotation, or "clearing," of the hips gives the downswing its rotary shape

After the weight shifts forward, the hips start rotating to the target.

and also preserves the resistance between the upper and lower halves created on the backswing. Maintaining this resistance well into the downswing allows you to unleash the power of the coil at impact.

By now the majority of the weight should be on the front foot. It's worth noting again that sequence

BEST TIP: *Attack from the Inside*

To groove an inside path into impact, practice hitting balls with your right foot pulled back 12 inches from its normal position and set on its toe. Make a normal swing from this stance and your right arm and shoulder will naturally drop to the inside as the swing changes direction, setting up a powerful in-to-out path through impact. Hit several balls from this stance and then try to incorporate the feeling into your normal swing.

—Jane Frost, *GOLF Magazine* Top 100 Teacher

of motion is crucial: Your lower body must lead the way, first with a lateral weight shift to the front foot, then with a rapid rotation of the hips. Since the hips turn fairly level, the unwinding force they create drops the club onto a flatter, more rotary plane, which brings the clubhead downward. This flattening of the swing plane sets up a powerful approach from the inside.

With the weight shifting forward, the left leg will serve as the axis around which the upper body turns through the ball, just as the right leg functioned on the backswing. This aggressive shifting and turning of the lower body clears a path for the hands and arms to deliver the club from the slot position—the key to strong, accurate ball-striking.

Narrowing of the Arc

A powerful swing features a distinct narrowing of the clubhead arc on the downswing. To understand this, consider a simple image. If the clubhead left a trail in the air like a skywriting plane, the downswing part of the trail, viewed from a face-to-face position with the golfer, would be much narrower, or closer to the body, than the backswing portion. It would look as if the golfer has yanked the grip in closer to his body on the downswing. This narrowing of the arc proves that the proper sequence of motion has occurred and also indicates stored power.

When the lower body leads the downswing, the right shoulder and arm are pulled downward, dropping the right elbow to the right side. Compare this position to its backswing counterpart and you'll notice there were several inches between the right elbow and the body going back, giving the backswing its wide, sweeping shape. By contrast, the right elbow virtually rides on the body coming down. Furthermore, the wrists are still fully cocked when the hands reach hip high in the downswing, which is exactly where the wrists *started* to cock on the backswing. This sharp wrist angle dramatically shortens the return path of the clubhead.

There is another reason the clubhead arc appears so much narrower on the downswing: the lateral shift of the hips. On aggressive full swings, the hips move about six inches toward the target at the start of the downswing—the "bump" I referred to earlier. This lateral move shifts the clubhead arc six inches forward. So, while the clubhead actually does stay closer to the body on the downswing, the repositioning of the lower body serves to exaggerate this narrowing effect.

> ## *BEST TIP: Check Your Width*
>
> To make sure you have the right sequence of motion on your downswing, compare your clubhead arc halfway down to its position halfway back. Set up next to a bush or small tree so that your clubhead just reaches the leaves halfway back. Then take some practice swings, stopping to check the clubhead position halfway down. Your lateral move toward the target to start the downswing and the subsequent body rotation should pull the clubhead at least a foot inside the leaves on the downswing.
>
> —Craig Shankland, *GOLF Magazine* Top 100 Teacher

Your Power Source

It's easy to say that brute force has no place in the golf swing. It's decidedly more difficult to sell this idea to a golfer who has just seen Tiger Woods or John Daly hit a tee shot. The explosion of power that these great players produce at impact makes it seem that they are attacking the ball with every ounce of energy they have.

Although they may be doing just that, it is important to remember that they are employing swinging force, not hitting force. That's the difference: The pros let the clubhead swing through the ball, while average golfers throw the club at the ball. Impact is not a position to the pros; it is simply an action that occurs between the backswing and the follow-through. To borrow an age-old saying, "The ball just gets in the way."

That's not to say that strength is not a power factor in golf. But upper-body strength typically associated with muscular people—the upper arms, chest, and shoulders—actually does little for the golf swing. The strength and flexibility of the trunk and the core muscles (abdomen and lower back) have a much greater impact

> ### Clubhead Follows Grip
> Wherever the grip end of the club points on the downswing is where the clubhead will swing through the hitting area. When the club drops into the slot, the butt end should point at the ball. As the swing continues, the butt should turn upward and point to the right of the target, indicating an on-plane swing and an approach from the inside. If the butt of the club points left of the target, the clubhead will swing out to in through impact, and the ball will tend to start to the left. If you slice, you probably suffer from this over-the-top move.

on your power potential than a muscular upper body. We've all seen our share of muscle-bound strongmen who can't hit the ball 200 yards off the tee. You wouldn't tell them they lack power—if you're smart—yet they are not powerful golfers.

So where does the power come from? Most of it is generated by the tension created as the upper body coils around the lower body. The more you can wind the torso against the resistance of the hips and legs, the more power you will store going back and then unleash coming down. This pivoting action of the body relies more on flexibility than strength: You'd much rather have elastic muscles that can produce the winding and unwinding motion than hulking muscles that limit your range of motion.

Other factors in creating power include weight transfer and your body's lever system. Driving your weight to the target on the downswing is critical because it initiates the uncoiling process and establishes the left side as the point of resistance for the full release of the right side through impact. As with so many aspects of the swing, weight transfer on the downswing is set up by the proper loading on the backswing. In other words, there's no weight to transfer if the backswing didn't do its job—yet another reason to focus on the early part of the swing.

BEST TIP: Towel Drill

Train yourself not to rush the club down from the top by making practice swings with a towel wrapped around the head of your driver. The air resistance of the towel trains you to build speed gradually on the downswing. With the uncoiling of your torso leading the way, the arms do not waste energy with an early hitting action and the clubhead achieves maximum speed through the bottom of the swing.

—Jeff Warne, *GOLF Magazine* Top 100 Teacher

As for your lever system, the biggest power producer is the wrist cock. When the wrists hinge on the backswing and create that 90-degree angle between the club and the left forearm, they store a tremendous amount of potential energy for the downswing. This is where so many golfers cheat themselves of power: They fully cock their wrists going back and then, in an attempt to create power, release this angle too early in the downswing with a hitting or swatting action. To take advantage of the power you've stored, you have to let centrifugal force unhinge the wrists, pull the left arm and the club into a straight line, and sling the clubhead into the ball. You have to simply let that happen.

Centrifugal force pulls the club in line with the left arm at impact.

The Moment of Truth

While it's true that the golf swing is an intricate chain of events, impact between clubhead and ball is the only position that really matters—the only position that the golf ball reacts to. Impact is when you either cash in on a well-timed, well-ordered move or you pay the piper for shortcuts or compensations taken along the way.

This being the case, you may be wondering why we've spent so much time discussing everything that precedes impact. Why not keep it simple and just describe where you need to be at impact? The answer is easy: because you have no conscious control over what the clubhead is doing when it collides with the

---

BEST TIP: *Extend for Power*

Power hitters maximize swing speed by making a full release of the club and a wide follow-through arc, the left wrist remaining flat and the left arm straight well past impact. To sense this extension, make some practice swings with your driver, letting your right hand slip off the grip as the clubhead approaches the hitting area. Without your right hand, your left arm will fully extend to the target and your left wrist will stay flat, as long as your body keeps rotating.

—T. J. Tomasi, *GOLF Magazine* Top 100 Teacher

ball. The swing is happening too quickly to manipulate the club in any reliable fashion. For this reason, the way you perform your downswing, your backswing, even your setup, is how you affect the position and speed of the clubhead as it reaches the ball.

There are, however, a few sensations you should be aware of through the impact area. First, make sure the clubhead is approaching from slightly inside the target line on a semicircle arc. In fact, on practice swings, you should be able to pick up the blurred path of the clubhead, even though it may be moving at speeds upwards of 100 mph at the bottom of the swing arc. Many good things have to happen in the downswing for the clubhead to approach on this path.

Next, you should feel like your right hand and arm are extending to the target. The old image for this is that you're skipping a stone across the surface of a pond with a sidearm motion, elbow leading the hand until the stone is released. To achieve this sensation, your left side must straighten up

Don't Return to Address

Forget the old instruction adage that says get into the same position at impact as you were at address. Although the clubhead must return to the ball, your knees and hips should be several inches closer to the target at impact, and your entire torso should be rotated well left. Think of impact as a driving, dynamic move to the target—a brief instant that sometimes eludes even the fastest cameras.

slightly to provide a point of resistance for the throwing action. Many teachers say you should feel like the right hand and arm make a slapping or spanking motion through the ball.

The important point to remember is that the entire right side should make an aggressive release through impact, aided by centrifugal force and the momen-

Through most of the downswing, the right elbow leads the right hand.

tum of the swing. The long-standing idea that the right side should be passive in the golf swing, so as not to overpower the left, does not apply in the hitting area. In short, no right-handed golfer should suppress the hitting power of his dominant side. Perhaps the legendary Ben Hogan put it best in *Five Lessons: The Modern Fundamentals of Golf* when he said, "As far as applying power goes, I wish that I had three right hands."

To the Finish

With the ball on its way, many golfers think the shot is over and their work is done. Well, you could argue that point, as you can't affect the fate of the ball after it leaves the clubface—despite any midair pleas or threats. You can, however, learn a lot from how you feel after impact and the positions you reach at the finish. Fact is, every motion in the golf swing flows into the follow-through, giving clues as to the correctness of the actions that got you there. Working backward from the finish is one of the most effective learning tools at your disposal.

Let's focus our analysis of the follow-through on three areas: weight transfer, body rotation, and arm swing. First, as you continue to push off the right side and onto the left, your head should remain in its starting position. In fact, it may even move slightly away from the target by impact to counter the driving force of the lower body through the strike. At the finish, all of your weight should be on the outside of your left foot, with your right foot on its toe and serving only to maintain balance.

The body rotation, as it has throughout the down-swing, follows the transfer of weight toward the target. The lower body continues to clear the way for the upper body, with the right side now powering the motion and pushing the body into the follow-through. At the finish, the right shoulder should be closer to the target than any other part of the body, and your belt buckle should point slightly left of the target, your chest even farther left. This fully rotated body position proves that the body pulls the arms and the club through impact—the key to maximum leverage and power.

As the body pulls the arms, the right side joins the party and applies some hitting force of its own. The

Heads Up

It's a good idea to let your head swivel in response to the shoulder turn, both on the backswing and down-swing. After impact, track your eyes down the target line after the streaking ball, instead of pulling up out of your posture. This will help you maintain your forward tilt through the shot to en-sure solid contact. In fact, two of today's top stars, David Duval and Annika Sorenstam, actually rotate their eyes down the line before impact, their heads swiveling, not lifting up.

Relaxed arms naturally rotate and extend through impact.

At the finish, the right shoulder is closest to the target.

right hand and arm fire through the strike, rotating the shaft as the right forearm rolls over the left. This is not a conscious action: If the hands and arms are free of excessive tension through the hitting area, they will naturally release the club. After impact, you should feel like the clubhead is chasing the ball to the target.

The momentum of the swing fully extends the arms toward the target, as the left elbow begins to fold, allowing the club to wrap around the body and run out of steam. One more good flowing sensation: The left elbow should point at the ground throughout the downswing and into the finish. If you can do this, the hands will float up to a position above the left shoulder, as you watch your ball soar to its target.

BEST TIP: Throw on a Scarf

To fully release your right hand and arm on the follow-through, imagine you're wrapping a scarf around your neck, throwing it with your right hand. Make some practice swings focusing on this image. It should promote the correct rotation of your right arm and also help keep it relaxed; a stiff right arm restricts your follow-through.

—Mitchell Spearman, *GOLF Magazine*
Top 100 Teacher

3

Chipping

Let's put some meaning to the "short" in short game. Here's the number-one rule in greenside play: Produce the "shortest" ball flight with the "shortest" possible swing that allows you to get the ball to the hole.

And what does that mean? It means keep the swing simple and get the ball rolling as soon as possible. If you can commit this concept to memory and recall it often, you'll save yourself countless strokes around the green. And that means lower scores, the quest for which no doubt has led you to this book.

Okay, so it's not quite that simple. Let me attach two conditions to our "short" philosophy. First, although you want the shortest ball flight, you should land the ball on the green whenever possible, where you'll get the most predictable bounce. Shoot to land the ball a yard or two onto the putting surface to allow some room for error on the short side.

The second condition involves the length of the swing. You want it to be as short as it can be, provided you maintain a smooth, natural rhythm from start to finish. In other words, don't make your backswing so short that you have to jerk the club on your downswing to get enough power. If you feel as if you have to help the club back down, your backswing is too short.

Let this rule, with its two conditions, guide your greenside play. If you do, you'll soon discover that most short shots can be run along the ground. Simply put, chipping is the backbone of the short game. It's the highest percentage play you can make, driven by a simple single-lever motion, with the left arm and the club essentially staying in a straight line from setup to finish. The swing is short and repeatable, and the ball flies low and rolls most of the way to the hole.

It's fitting that our analysis start with the standard chip shot. It may not be the most exciting shot in the game, but it is the easiest to learn and the safest to employ. In the words of the immortal Bobby Jones, "The chip is the great economist of golf."

What Is a Chip?

The first step in becoming a smarter, more effective player around the greens is understanding your options, understanding the difference between a chip, a pitch, a lob, and so on. Once you know the characteristics of each shot, you can confidently choose among them in a given situation, knowing that you have picked the right play. Such confidence breeds success.

The chip shot is generally thought to be any short shot that flies no more than a third of its total distance and rolls at least two thirds. Keep in mind these are the outside parameters that apply when chipping with a wedge; chips played with a short or middle iron can roll as much as five or six times farther than they carry in the air.

The chip shot comes with little risk. Its objective is to bump the ball out of the grass and onto the edge of the green. Except for a putt, it's the simplest motion in golf, and the simpler the motion, the less the chance of something going wrong. Add this to

The chip shot rolls at least two-thirds of its total distance.

the fact that a rolling ball is more predictable than a flying ball that can still take a bad hop when it lands, and you'll understand why the chip should be your first greenside choice.

The putting stroke is even safer, but putting from off the green requires an excellent lie and smooth ground the whole way. Otherwise, the chip is a better bet. Remember, your objective should be to minimize risk: Putt before you chip; chip before you pitch; pitch before you lob. Keep that in mind and you're on your way to getting the most out of your game around the greens.

When Not to Chip

For all its good qualities, there are times when a chip shot is the wrong choice. If you have to carry the ball more than a third of the way to the hole due to intervening obstacles, such as deep rough or sand, you should play a more lofted shot. The worst swing thought you can have around the green is that you have to help the ball into the air to land safely on the green. When this notion crosses your mind, stop and rethink your shot.

Likewise, when hitting to an elevated green, you may need more height than a standard chip provides to carry the ball onto the putting surface. Try-

BEST TIP: Grip-Down Drill

Good chipping demands firm wrists through impact and free body rotation back and through. To ingrain these fundamentals, practice your chipping motion with your hands choked down to the shaft and the butt of the grip touching your left side. Keeping the grip against your ribs, swing the clubhead back and through in the air, noting how your wrists remain stable and your body turns back and through with the swinging motion.

—Carl Welty, *GOLF Magazine* Top 100 Teacher

ing to bounce your ball into or up a slope is unpredictable. Plan your first bounce to be on the putting surface itself, where the ground usually is more level and the grass is uniform.

Sometimes a poor lie in deep rough also makes a chip shot inadvisable, since the ball needs to come out high enough to keep from getting snagged by the long grass. In fact, even when the ball itself is sitting up, the grass around it must be considered: A clump of thick grass behind the ball may require a steeper downswing than the standard chip provides, and long grass in front of the ball may require a higher launch angle off the clubface.

BEST TIP: Learn to rotate your body and keep your wrists firm by choking up on a club and swinging with the grip against your left side.

So, the chip shot is not the be-all and end-all of the short game, but it should be your favorite option around the green. Whenever putting is unwise—and it often is—set your sights on chipping. If you can't make a strong case *against* chipping, you have a strong case *for* it.

How to Plan a Chip

Chip-shot execution should begin as soon as your previous shot comes to rest. Say you've missed your approach shot to the right and your ball finds an uphill lie just off a slick downhill green. The best view of this shot is probably on your walk up to the green: You can see the nature of the terrain from start to finish, where the ball should land, the incline of the lie, and the decline of the green. These subtleties are tough to judge once you're at the ball. Take full advantage of your perspective on your walk to the green.

Once you reach the ball, develop a picture in your mind as to how you want the shot to look: the bounce, the roll, the final destination. Crouch down behind the ball and read the shot like you would a putt, first picking a spot on the green for the initial bounce. Remember, this landing spot should be at least a yard onto the green to provide room for error if you catch the shot a bit heavy or thin.

Next comes club selection. There are two schools of thought on how to pick a club for chipping. One theory says develop a comfort level with a single club, say a pitching wedge, and use it for all your chip shots, adjusting the length of the swing to dictate the distance of the shot. The other theory advocates a single swing for chipping that produces different shots with different clubs, anything from a sand wedge to a 5-iron. Both are reliable methods, although changing clubs rather than adjusting your swing to produce different results is a simpler approach.

We'll get into the mechanics of the setup and swing in a moment, but first consider two preshot factors that grow in importance as you get closer to the hole: precision and relaxation. Simply put, the shorter the shot, the greater your expectation of precision. For example, if you miss a green with a 3-iron, you may not be all that upset; but if you leave a little chip shot in the long grass, you want to bite the club in half. That's because you've fallen miserably short of your expectations.

As for relaxation, shorter shots require less big-muscle motion and therefore rely more on your sense of rhythm and timing. Tension is rhythm's

To bolster feel, make swings looking down the line.

biggest enemy, making it critical to ward off stress on short shots. To do this, commit to the shot and club you've chosen and focus on executing what you see in your mind's eye. Make a few rehearsal swings in a similar lie, looking down the line and sensing the effort required, then step up and hit the ball. Don't waste time second-guessing your decisions. Extra time means extra tension. Envision, commit, rehearse, and execute.

Chipping Setup

The basic motion of the chip shot is a downward hit, the clubface contacting the ball before the club has reached the bottom of its downswing arc. This descending action is preferred because the most important factor in chipping is clean clubface-to-ball contact, and the most reliable method for doing this is making contact while the clubhead is still in its descent. Think of it as pinching the ball against the turf.

Clean contact in chipping is critical for two reasons: First, catching grass before the ball on a chipping swing kills the momentum of the clubhead, often cutting power significantly before it reaches the ball; and second, when grass gets trapped be-

---

Free Chips

Next time you're walking down the fairway with your wedge in hand, stop for a minute and take a few practice chipping swings, trying to brush a leaf or loose grass off the turf. You'll be surprised how smooth and rhythmic your stroke is without the prospect of a difficult shot in front of you. Try to internalize this fluid action and recall it the next time you face an intimidating chip shot.

tween the clubface and the ball, the nature of the contact and the spin imparted on the ball is unpredictable. Catching grass first may work out on full shots, where the clubhead often tears through the grass with little effect, but when playing from short range, you simply cannot take the chance of making poor contact.

Every aspect of the standard chipping setup is designed to promote a descending blow and a low, running shot that lands just on the green and rolls to the hole. Here are the specifics:

Play the ball back.   Position the ball opposite your right instep and push your hands toward the target, until they're even with your left thigh. This hands-ahead position sets up a steep backswing and a descending motion at impact, with the hands leading the clubhead until well after the ball is gone.

Set your weight left.   Place 60 to 70 percent of your body weight on your left foot at address. This further encourages a downward angle of approach but also discourages weight transfer during the swing by presetting the weight on the target side, where it has to end up. Weight transfer is an unnecessary complication in chipping.

For a standard chip, set the ball back and your weight left.

Take a narrow stance.   With your heels six to eight inches apart, you'll naturally resist weight movement during the swing. Keeping the feet close together also sets you more upright and therefore nearer the ball, which increases your control of the motion, as your hands and arms stay closer to the body.

Choke down for feel.   Slide your hands down the grip until your right hand is almost to the end of the handle. This effectively shortens the club, which reduces the power of the swing and bolsters control.

Set up square to slightly open.   A square stance makes sense, as it promotes a straight clubhead path through impact, but some golfers like to open up a bit to gain a better view of the line. This is a matter of preference: If you feel comfortable standing open, it can be beneficial, but if you find yourself hitting chips off-line, by all means use a square setup.

Square the clubface.   As you move the ball back in your stance, the tendency will be to flare the clubface open. And unless you make an in-swing compensation, you all but guarantee an open clubface at impact, which will send the ball right of your intended line. To guard against this, always make sure the leading edge, or bottom, of your clubface is perpendicular to your starting line, regardless of ball position. Then you can swing away knowing your clubface will be square when it meets the ball.

BEST TIP: Looking Ahead

In chipping, a slight lean toward the target at address promotes a steep downswing and clean contact with the ball. To create this leaning action, focus your eyes on the front half of the ball as you take your stance. This will ensure that your head is slightly in front of the ball and that the shaft is angled toward the target. From there, the backswing will be fairly upright, setting up a descending blow and crisp contact.

—Laird Small, *GOLF Magazine* Top 100 Teacher

Chipping Swing

You've no doubt heard the term "one-piece takeaway" to describe the first move away from the ball in the full swing. Well, this concept of starting the

arms, shoulders, and club in a unified, synchronized motion is a great mental image for the chipping swing as well—not only on the takeaway, but
throughout the entire motion.

Picture the chipping setup just described or, better yet, take your address facing a full-length mirror. You'll notice your arms and shoulders form a
large triangle—each arm being a side and the line
of your shoulders representing the third side. The
key to good chipping is keeping this triangle intact
from the setup to the finish, meaning it should not
change shape as you swing away from the ball or
through to the target. This demands that the shoulders turn at the same rate that the arms swing.

The age-old concept that chipping is a hands-and-
arms motion is dead wrong. The small muscles of
the hands, wrists, and forearms are the least reliable
actors in the golf swing, particularly under pressure,
and therefore should be prohibited from leading
any motion. Instead, think of the chipping swing as
a mini-turn back and a mini-turn through—a one-
piece motion all the way.

Here's the basic technique for chipping:

Start relaxed. Tension in the hands, arms, or
body at address virtually guarantees a quick start,

from which a chipping swing will rarely recover. To prevent tension and encourage a smooth first move, hover the clubhead at address, slowly wagging it back and forth as you track your eyes down the line. Watch Raymond Floyd, one of the game's best chippers, as he stands over chip shots; he looks as if he's drawing circles in the air with his clubhead.

Swing triangle back.

Keeping your weight left and your head stock-still, move the hands, arms, and shoulders away from the ball as a single unit. This is a pendulum-type motion similar to putting, where no part of the swing outraces any other and the body center stays firmly in place.

Let the body react.

Although you shouldn't consciously hinge your wrists during the chipping swing, they should be free to react naturally to the swinging of the club. This will happen automatically if you keep your grip soft. As for your lower body, it should also feel relaxed and responsive. The knees and hips should rotate back slightly in reaction to the swinging motion, without any thought on your part.

The arms and shoulders swing the club back together.

Reverse the motion. The downswing should be a mirror image of the backswing. If you've started from a good setup position, you need not think about making the downward blow required in chipping. Simply swing the arms-and-shoulders triangle to the target, letting the clubhead naturally accelerate through impact.

Let the clubhead accelerate through the strike.

Finish to the target. Assuming you have a decent lie, there should be nothing choppy in your chipping motion. Swing the clubhead through at least as far as you swung it back, never letting your wrists flip or your shoulders stop rotating. At the finish, the clubhead should be about shin-high and your upper body should be half-turned toward the target.

4

Sand Play

Let's get something straight: Most amateurs are pathetic in the sand—and they know it. You may think you're a decent chipper; maybe you can even pitch the ball with a fair bit of confidence. But if you're like most golfers, you'd rather find your ball buried in six-inch rough than staring at you from a greenside bunker.

The simple truth is that most poor bunker play stems from a lack of understanding of what needs to happen at impact. You don't have to dig halfway to China to blast the ball out. In fact, the deeper you try to dig the better your chances of taking too much sand and—dare I say—leaving it in the bunker. The only thing worse than not getting out of the sand the first time is having the chance to do it over again.

So why do the pros look so darned comfortable in the sand? Because they know two advantages that sand shots have over other greenside shots: predictability and forgiveness. First, the pros know sand is a fairly predictable playing surface from one shot to the next, in terms of both firmness and depth. Assuming your ball is sitting on top of the sand, you know what lies underneath it. That's where you're guessing with other lies; even in seemingly good lies in the grass, you never know how firm it is underneath. You don't have that uncertainty when you're in the sand.

The second reason pros like sand is that it is forgiving; it leaves room for error. Since your clubface never comes in contact with the ball on bunker shots, solid contact—perhaps your biggest fear in other greenside shots—is simply not an issue. In fact, with the right swing, you can enter the sand an inch or so closer to or farther from the ball than you planned and still produce a decent shot. Where else can you say that around the green?

So before you conclude that you'll never be much of a bunker player, read through the instruction that follows. It's a lot simpler than you may think, and could easily become a strength in your game. Maybe you'll start wishing for bunker shots,

No Choking

For most golfers, sand means tension. And the first place tension rears its ugly head is in the grip, where the fingers strangle the handle and send pressure up the arms and into the body. The usual result is a fast, jerky swing and inconsistent shots. To nip tension in the bud, "milk" the handle at address, exerting and releasing pressure with your fingers. Don't take the club back until your grip feels soft. Only then are you ready to go.

like the pros sometimes do—or at least not feel as if you're doomed when your ball ends up on the beach.

How to Plan a Bunker Shot

Most golfers climb into bunkers with a fair amount of mental baggage. Each can tell you horror stories of disaster holes or career rounds ended in the sand. And every one of us can commiserate. But those are harmful thoughts as you step up to a bunker shot. You need a clear, confident approach and a simple plan of attack.

First, be thankful that the two major decisions you usually have to make next to the green—shot selection and club selection—are no-brainers in the sand. The basic bunker technique I'm about to discuss works for most greenside sand shots, and the sand wedge should be your weapon of choice in

A simple plan and positive visualization are crucial in bunker play.

A club has "bounce" if the trailing edge of the sole is lower than the leading edge.

virtually every situation. (Due to its "bounce" feature, the sand wedge slides through the sand instead of digging.) So, there are two fewer things to think about. And you thought this was hard?

Your first order of business, assuming you have a decent lie, is deciding where you want to hit the shot. This may sound obvious, but you don't always want to play directly to the hole. For instance, if you're staring at the tallest part of the bunker lip or you have deep trouble directly behind the hole, you may want to look for a safer route. That decision hinges on how much confidence you have in your sand game. But for most players, it's better to be thinking about getting on the green, not getting to the hole.

Once you know where you're going, pick a landing area. It may be difficult to zero in on a specific spot, but figure out the general area where you want the ball to touch down. This gives you something positive to focus on, rather than bad memories or the opportunity for disaster that the shot presents. Simply pick your shot, then your spot, and keep your thoughts focused and positive.

Although we're about to look at setup and swing mechanics, bunker play is largely about feel. Swinging through the sand produces a much different sensation than hitting the ball directly; you should pre-sense how you want your body and the club to feel as you prepare to hit the shot. Focus less on the technique of the swing and more on how the club should move through the impact area. As you become a better bunker player, you'll rely almost totally on your instincts in the sand.

One last point on preparation: Check your tension level. Negative thoughts and fear cause tension, which tightens the grip and quickens the swing. Take a few deep breaths and shake out your hands. And remember, try to draw on the good experiences you've had, not the heartbreakers.

Bunker Setup

First, realize that the prevailing technique used in bunker play has changed. Traditional instruction says the bunker swing is a steep, out-to-in swipe that slices across the line, digging under the ball and popping it out of the sand. Today, most instructors teach a shallower swing that slides the club-

---

BEST TIP: Predictable Roll

Tour pros rarely use the traditional out-to-in swing for bunker shots. We know it imparts a lot of left-to-right sidespin on the ball, which can be difficult to plan for on the landing. Instead, we prefer a more normal swing path, the clubhead cutting a swath in the sand that points to the target. Picture a rectangle in the sand with the ball in the middle and make a steep swing back and through, trying to slice the entire rectangle out of the sand. A straight swing will produce a straight roll.

—Curtis Strange, two-time
U.S. Open Champion

---

head just under the surface of the sand and clips the ball off the top. This new method has proven to be more effective and more forgiving.

As a result of this change in thinking, the traditional bunker setup has also undergone an overhaul. The old stance was dramatically open, with the feet sunk deep in the sand, to promote a backswing to the outside and a steep, explosive descent into the ball. The new setup is designed to let you move the clubhead in a normal swing arc, from the inside coming down and back to the inside on the follow-through. This path creates a shallower approach to the ball and a longer, thinner cut in the sand.

The following setup keys will put you in position to execute the modern bunker shot.

Open the clubface. This exposes the bounce on the bottom of the sole and adds loft to the clubface. However, you should open the face before you step into the bunker: With your left hand on the grip, rotate the club clockwise about 20 degrees with your right hand and then take your normal grip with both hands. If you merely turn the clubface open at address, without changing your hand positions, you haven't really opened the clubface at all.

Play the ball forward. Since you actually want to make fat contact, touching down in the sand first, position the ball about an inch in front of the center of your stance. Let your arms hang naturally; your hands should be slightly behind the ball at address, the shaft tilting neither toward nor away from the target. This promotes a fairly level swipe through the sand, with the ball in the middle of your sand divot.

Take a wider stance. Even if you dig your feet in, your stance in a bunker is never rock-solid due to the shifting nature of the sand. To create a steady base, spread your feet apart so your insteps are at hip-width. You still won't be able to transfer much weight or move laterally off the ball, which will do wonders for your consistency. Your objective is to make a smooth, accelerating swing while staying in perfect balance.

Align slightly open. Shift your stance, as well as your knees, hips, and shoulders, about 20 degrees open to the target. This open position presets a full rotation of the body through the shot, a move that many amateurs fail to make in the sand. Once your

For a standard shot, play the ball just ahead of center.

feet are positioned, twist them down into the sand about an inch, which lowers your entire body and therefore the bottom of the swing arc. Remember, you want the swing to bottom out in the sand under the ball, not at ball level.

Aim an inch behind the ball. You
actually want to contact the sand about two or
three inches behind the ball, but if you aim the
leading edge about an inch behind it, the bounce
factor of your sand wedge will cause the trailing
edge to enter the sand first. But try not to get too
stuck on this aiming point: If you make it the
focus of the entire swing, you'll probably fail to
swing the clubhead through the sand—a common
amateur mistake.

BEST TIP: Dial the Face

Control the depth of your divot holes in the
sand by increasing or decreasing the angle of
the flange—the clubhead's protruding sole. The
more you open the clubface—also known as
"dialing the face"—the greater the angle of the
flange, which prevents you from digging too
deep in the sand. I like to play most of my
bunker shots with the leading edge pointing toward 1:30 or 2 o'clock. This shallows out the
divot and adds loft and spin to the shot.

—Phil Rodgers, *GOLF Magazine*
Top 100 Teacher

Bunker Swing

Many golfers feel as if they have to manufacture a totally different swing when they step into the sand. They try to make a steep, out-to-in motion that they use nowhere else on the golf course. This is a mistake.

Truth is, anyone who can make a simple pitch swing can hit a good bunker shot—and that means any golfer. The motion is essentially the same: Swing the club and turn the body in one motion, then move everything through together. The fact that you're hitting sand instead of a golf ball should not affect the swing; the only difference is that the bunker swing needs to be longer and faster to hit the ball the same distance as a normal pitch shot. Practice will tell you how far your standard bunker shot travels compared to your standard pitch.

Hank Johnson, one of *GOLF Magazine*'s Top 100 Teachers, discusses this relationship in his book *How to Win the Three Games of Golf:* "I usually count on a 3-to-1 ratio. A swing that would hit a standard pitch 30 yards would hit a bunker shot 10 yards. A stroke that would send a standard pitch 60 yards would result in a 20-yard bunker shot."

Relating your bunker swing to your pitching swing should be helpful: It's a move away from the old out-to-in method, and should help dispel the mystique of sand play by linking it to something with which you're more comfortable.

Here are the swing keys for a standard greenside bunker shot:

Hover the clubhead. Be thankful for the rule that prohibits you from grounding your clubhead in the sand. By having to support the weight of the club at address, you sustain a constant grip pressure, which promotes a smooth, unhurried takeaway. Given the tension that most golfers feel in the sand, it's also a good idea to waggle the clubhead back and forth or up and down to quiet stress in the hands and arms.

Start the arms and shoulders together.
Make a one-piece takeaway, turning your shoulders as your arms swing the club on a slightly inside path. Let the wrists hinge the club upward, an action that will happen naturally provided your grip is light and your wrists are supple. Think of the lower body as the base of the

swing: The hips and legs should support the actions of the arms and torso, responding to motion, not creating motion.

Make a three-quarter backswing.

Lengthening your backswing is the best way to promote more clubhead speed coming down so you can power through the sand. At the top, your wrists should be fully hinged, the club at a right angle to your left arm, and your hands should be at about shoulder height. Also, make a three-quarter body turn away from the ball, with your back almost to the target and your left shoulder nearly under your chin. These backswing positions set up a proper move into impact.

Turn and swing through impact.

From the top, turn your body and swing your arms down in one synchronized movement. Provided your arms don't rush out in front, the club will track back down to the ball on an inside path, producing a shallow entry into the sand and a long, thin divot. The old out-to-in technique produces bomb craters because the downswing is a steep motion controlled mainly by the arms. Today's method features more

Make a three-quarter backswing with a full wrist hinge.

Cut a shallow divot and keep the clubhead moving.

body rotation back and through, which shallows out the swing and helps the clubhead slip through the sand, rather than slam into it.

Continue to a three-quarter finish. The shallower swing arc allows you to swing through

At the finish, the chest should be turned to the target.

the sand with less resistance and therefore achieve a fuller finish. Your clubhead should touch down two to three inches behind the ball and slide underneath it. As a result, the ball will fly out on a pillow of sand without ever making contact with the clubface. Impact should be a muffled "thump," like the sound of beating out an old rug. At the finish, your chest should face the target, indicating full body rotation on the downswing.

BEST TIP: How to Vary Distance

Many amateurs have trouble varying distance on bunker shots. Part of the problem is how they finish: They swing into a full follow-through regardless of the shot at hand. As a rule, the length of the follow-through should correspond to the length of the shot. A short shot needs a short follow-through, and a long shot needs a long follow-through. You wouldn't finish with the club up over your shoulder on a short pitch shot; so don't do it for a short bunker shot either. Match your finish to the shot you need.

—Martin Hall, *GOLF Magazine*
Master Teaching Professional

5

Putting: The Setup

Any discussion of putting technique has to begin with two acknowledgments. The first one is that at the end of the day, there is no "right" way to putt. Because putting is such a make-or-break part of the game, whatever happens to get the ball in the hole in the least number of strokes is perfect. If you digest all the information in this book and then realize that you're deadly from inside 10 feet standing on one foot, stick with it. That technique is right for you. On the Tour, making putts is the difference between big money and just scraping by. So it's not surprising to see a wide variety of putting styles among the pros, from tall posture to crouched posture, from narrow to wide stances, from short, poppy strokes to long, slow sweeps. Players do what works.

Second acknowledgment: Even though there are no hard-and-fast rules of putting technique, there are a handful of fundamentals that work for most golfers. Those fundamentals will be the primary focus of the technical section of this book. More specifically, most golfers will find the greatest success by making a putting stroke that is controlled almost entirely by moving the arms and shoulders as a unit, while the hands simply follow along. *For most golfers,* it's easier to keep the putterface pointed at the target if the hands and wrists aren't doing anything except stabilizing the club.

For sure, there have been great putters who used wristy strokes—and "alternative techniques" will also be addressed in the book—but most of the fundamentals of grip, stance, and alignment are designed to promote an arms-and-shoulders stroke, because that's the simplest way to do it. And simple means easy to do well, and easy to repeat. So, before you jump to the conclusion that your stroke is decidedly idiosyncratic, get to know and understand these basic fundamentals. See how they work for you. If you're a better player, use them to check yourself. A prolonged stretch of inconsistency might indicate that you've wandered too far away from them. But no matter your level of play, let simplicity be the foundation of your putting stroke. Once that's established, you can go about discovering the nuances that will make your stroke distinctly yours.

The Pendulum Motion

Imagine a tower with a pendulum hanging from a fixed point at the top, like a grandfather clock. The pendulum swings back and forth while the clock tower remains still. It's a time-worn yet perfect analogy for an arms-and-shoulders putting stroke. Your body is the tower, and your shoulders, arms, hands, and putter form the pendulum. The fixed point is right between your shoulders—the very top of your sternum. The body remains still while the shoulders, arms, hands, and club swing back and through. If you think in those terms, it's easy to see why grip and stance are such important parts of putting. If your hands and wrists move independently, the pendulum breaks down. If your stance is unstable, the pendulum won't swing from a fixed point.

You can see and feel the pendulum motion by standing in front of a full-length mirror without a golf club. Bend forward from the hips and clap your palms together so your hands, arms, and shoulders form a large triangle (remember this triangle image, as we'll come back to it often). Keeping the palms together, swing the arms back and through by rocking the shoulders. Notice how the triangle is maintained throughout the motion; the relationship between the hands, arms, and shoulders never changes. This is the

To feel the pendulum, swing your hands and arms back as a triangle.

essence of the arms-and-shoulders stroke; it changes slightly when there's an actual club in your hands, but your grip and stance should be designed to make the difference as small as possible.

As you swing through, maintain the shape of the triangle.

Grip

When the palms face each other directly below your sternum, as they do when you create the triangle, they are perpendicular to the target line. In other words, the back of the left hand and the palm of the right hand face the hole, which makes it easier to swing the arms back and through on a straight line. That's the goal with the putting grip; there are many different variations, but you'll find it easiest to make a straight arms-and-shoulders stroke if the palms face each other.

Fortunately, most putter grips are designed to help you do this. Find the flat ridge running down the middle of the grip; if you hold the club with both thumbs resting on top of that ridge, your palms will be effectively facing each other. (The palms don't *really* face each other, not as they do in the triangle exercise, because the right hand is below the left on the grip.) Generally, the hands are closer together on the putter than they are in a regular full-swing grip. That way, they operate much more as a single unit, keeping the connection between the arms and putter as seamless as possible so the pendulum can swing without any unnecessary complications.

In the traditional Vardon, or overlapping, grip used in the full swing, the club sits in the fingers of

The grip should run down the middle of the left palm.

the left hand, allowing the wrist the necessary mobility to hinge during the swing. With a putter, however, the grip is nestled into the palm of the hand, locked right into the channel created by the thumb pad and the heel. Holding the handle in the palm not only points the back of the hand to the target, but has the effect of immobilizing the left wrist as well, so the swinging of the putter can be a natural extension of the arms-and-shoulders movement. (Incidentally, this is why some players prefer a thicker grip on their putters—it makes it easier to grip in the palm, thereby reducing the risk of unwanted contribution from the hands and wrists.) The left thumb sits on top of the grip, on the flat ridge, and, although the fingers should never apply more than moderate pressure to the handle, the bulk of the squeezing in the left hand is done by the last two fingers.

Place the right hand on the grip so the right thumb pad covers the left thumb and the right thumb rests on the flat ridge. Wrap all four fingers of the right hand around the handle so the palm directly faces the target. In the reverse-overlap grip—the accepted "standard" for putting—the left forefinger, and sometimes the middle finger, too, rests on top of the fingers of the right hand. It's this overlapping of fingers that makes it possible for the hands to be as close together as possible. First try overlapping the left forefinger only. Does the grip feel as if it's seated securely in your left palm between the heel and thumb pad? If it doesn't, you

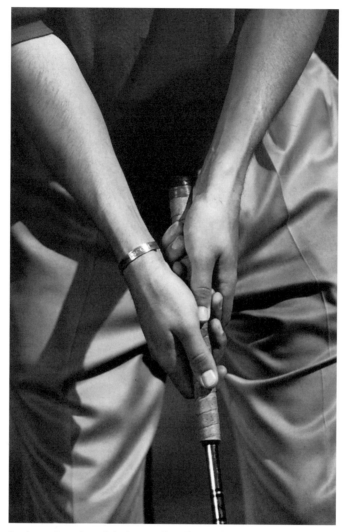

Both thumbs should sit on the flat ridge on top of the grip.

can try extending the left forefinger so it points down the shaft, across the first knuckles of the fingers of the right hand. Let the middle finger of the left hand overlap the pinkie or ring finger of the

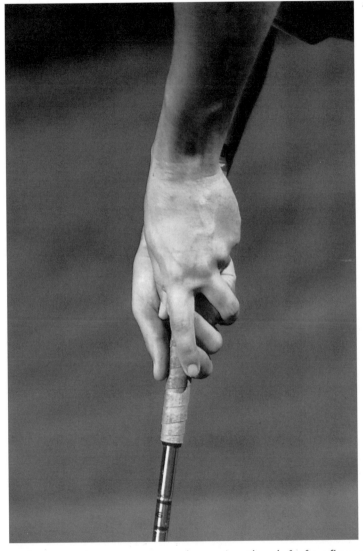

In the popular reverse-overlap grip, the left forefinger "overlaps" the right hand.

right. You may find it easier to set the grip in the palm of the left hand this way. Certainly with two fingers overlapping, the hands are closer together. If you feel like you can control the putter with this grip, it's a great way to keep the hands operating as a single unit.

Already you can see that there are viable options when it comes to gripping the putter. If you decide to experiment, remember the goals of a conventional grip: to keep the hands close together, the palms facing each other, and wrist action to a minimum. With a good grip, you have in place the critical first piece of the putting puzzle.

First and Foremost

The reverse-overlap grip was invented by Walter J. Travis, a putting pioneer who won three of the first four U.S. Amateur Championships of the 20th century. A late bloomer who didn't take up the game until his mid-30s, Travis was a notoriously short hitter who compensated by infuriating his opponents with stellar putting. Nobody complained about his grip (he later taught it to the great Bobby Jones), but his putter—one of the first center-shafted models, known as "The Schenectady"—was banned in Britain after he won the 1904 British Amateur.

Stance and Posture

Like the hands, the position of the body has a major effect on your ability to make a straight, smooth pendulum stroke. Go back to the triangle exercise: If you stand perfectly straight and tall, there won't be any room for your arms to swing back and through; your body will be in the way. Similarly, if your stance points 45 degrees to the left, your arms will want to swing that way, instead of to the target. Positioning the body to putt is not a complicated process, but it is something to be meticulous about. Good body position breeds a good stroke; poor position breeds compensations and mistakes.

In a standard putting stroke, only the pendulum moves—the shoulders, arms, and hands. The rest of the body—legs, hips, torso, head—remains still from the moment the stroke starts until after contact is made. You should always be relaxed, but at the same time, your stance serves to lock your body into place.

Start without a club. Stand with your feet 15 to 20 inches apart and square to the target line (imagine a line drawn across the tops of your toes; if that line is parallel to the line running from the ball to the target, your stance is square). Stability is the prime objective here, so distribute your weight evenly between each foot and allow the knees to flex slightly. Locking the knees may feel stable, but it actually creates tension in the body, which will eventually creep into your stroke. Bend forward slightly from the hips; notice how this allows the arms to hang from the shoulders, away from the torso. If you feel your weight moving onto your toes, you're bending too far.

This posture puts the body in position to make a straight-back, straight-through pendulum stroke. It's a square setup—if you drew imaginary lines across the feet, knees, hips, and shoulders, all would be parallel to the target line. Also, notice

With proper posture, the hands hang below the shoulders.

from a down-the-line view how the hands hang under the shoulders. That way, they can easily swing straight back and through on a line parallel to the target line.

Now try it with a putter and a ball. Everything stays the same: feet square, knees slightly flexed, torso bent forward from the hips, hands directly under shoulders . . . plus one more thing. Draw an-

A square stance promotes an on-line stroke.

other imaginary line—this time from your eyes to the ball. That line should be vertical, or very close to vertical, indicating that your eyes are over the ball. This is a must if you're going to see the line of the putt clearly. Otherwise, you're looking at the line from an odd angle, which will distort your perception. Generally, if your eyes are well inside the ball, what appears to be a straight line at the hole will actually point to the right of the hole; if the eyes are outside the ball, what appears to be a straight line will actually point to the left. Only if your eyes are over the ball can you be sure that what you see is what you actually get.

BEST TIP: Stay Balanced

Here are two quick ways to make sure that your body is balanced at the setup, with the arms hanging naturally from the shoulders: 1. If you lift the putter off the ground slightly, it should remain in place, not drift one way or another; 2. Have a friend try to push you off balance. If you're set up properly, it shouldn't have much effect. If you stumble, you weren't very stable in your setup.

—Gregor Jamieson, *GOLF Magazine*
Top 100 Teacher

BEST TIP: Check Your Eyeline

You can be sure that your eyes are over the ball by dropping a second ball from the bridge of your nose; it should hit the ball you're addressing. But it's just as important that your eyeline be parallel to the target line. To check this, take your stance, then hold your putter horizontally at waist level so it is directly under your eyes. If your eyes are over the ball, the shaft should appear to cover the ball; and you know your eyeline is parallel to the target line when you swivel your head and see that the shaft points directly at the hole.

—Eddie Merrins, *GOLF Magazine*
Top 100 Teacher

Arnie's Unusual Stance

How important is it for your body to be stable? If you go by the great Arnold Palmer, at his best one of the top pressure putters ever, a still body is crucial, no matter what the cost. Palmer was an athletic, charismatic player when his aggressive style of play captured the world's imagination in the 1950s and '60s, but he looked rather unconventional doing it. His full swing was a fast, swiping motion, and his putting stance looked as if he was a long way from a bathroom—and knew it. Knees knocked, feet pigeon-toed, thighs pinched together, he bent way over from the hips to get close to the ball. It wasn't pretty, but it served to lock his body into place so the only thing moving during the stroke would be his shoulders, arms, and hands. And the results he achieved speak for themselves.

Square vs. Open

It's simplest to putt with your feet—and the rest of your body—perfectly parallel to the target line, but it's not uncommon to see good players adopting an open stance, in which an imaginary line drawn across the feet angles to the left of the target. Two of the best putters in history, Jack Nicklaus and Ben Crenshaw, have frequently used an open stance, claiming that it makes it easier to see the line of the putt. While that may be true, understand that if your feet are angled to the left of the target, your shoulders probably will be, as well. This alignment will then encourage your arms to swing in the same direction—to the left. Given that, the only way to swing the putterhead straight down the target line is to reroute it with the hands and arms during the stroke, which is probably more complication than you want to add to your putting motion.

Nicklaus and Crenshaw pulled it off because both had razor-sharp touch in their prime, but for the average golfer, it's much more practical to adopt a square stance. With a square setup, the arms can just follow the lead of the shoulders, without any extra manipulation required.

To Crouch or Not to Crouch

How much should you crouch over when you putt? Again, look at Nicklaus and Crenshaw: Jack always crouched as much as anybody on Tour, while Ben stood tall. Both, obviously, can be fantastic ways to putt. But keep this in mind: Crouching gets you closer to the ball, which can offer a better sense of control, but it also creates angles in the elbows and wrists. For some, those angles can destabilize the triangle formed by the shoulders, arms, and hands, so the shoulders are no longer in complete control of the stroke.

Standing tall, on the other hand, allows the arms to hang straight, or nearly straight, from the shoul-

Crouching over can bolster feel but complicate the stroke.

ders. Being farther from the ball doesn't provide the same sense of control, but you may find it easier to make a smooth pendulum stroke if the arms and wrists are essentially straight and the integrity of the triangle is maintained. Experiment to find what feels best for you.

Standing tall can simplify the stroke but may reduce feel.

The Importance of Ball Position

All theories aside, the putting stroke is not a perfect pendulum motion. In order for that to happen, the putter would have to be built like a croquet mallet, so the arms and shaft could form a vertical line down from the shoulders to the ball. And the shoulders would have to make a perfectly vertical rocking motion, like a hanger on a coat rack.

In reality, the putter is more like a hockey stick, with the shaft angled toward the player. Also, the shoulders don't rock on a perfectly vertical line; they rotate around the spine, as they do in the full swing. As a result, the motion that the putterhead makes during the stroke is *pendulum-like*, but also slightly rounded. That is, not only does the putterhead lift off the ground as it swings back, it also moves slightly to the inside of the target line. As it swings through, it returns down to the target line, then swings up and through to the inside again. It's not very pronounced, and in most cases, it's not even noticeable, but that rounded path is precisely why ball position is critical.

Consider how this path affects the angle of the putterface. When the putterhead goes back slightly inside the line, the putterface naturally rotates open relative to the target. It returns to square at the bottom of the swing arc, stays square for a couple of inches, then rotates closed to the target as the putterhead swings through. So, all else being equal, unless you make contact when the putterhead is within a couple of inches of the bottom of the swing arc, the ball will not roll on the line you've intended. And that's not all. In order for the ball to roll as smoothly as possible, contact must be made when the putterhead is moving parallel to the ground or just slightly on the upswing. If contact is made too early or too late, the ball may skid excessively or hop before rolling, both of which can affect distance control. In other words, you can make a perfect stroke and still miss—and miss badly—if you haven't positioned the ball in your stance correctly.

The good news is that the legs and torso don't move during the stroke, so the low point of the swing arc will generally be in the same place relative to your body every time. To find that spot, go back to the pendulum; the low point of a pendulum's arc is opposite the fixed point where the top of the pendulum connects to the tower. Now think in terms of the triangle exercise: The fixed point is a spot between your shoulders, at the top of the sternum. When the hands are directly under that spot, they are at the bottom of the swing arc. That should be your reference point when positioning your body to the ball.

The putterface should make contact at the low point or just slightly ahead of it (remember, you've got a two-inch window before the putterface begins to rotate off-line). So, position the ball just ahead of the middle of your sternum, about an inch. Assuming your weight is evenly distributed between both feet, that's far enough forward to ensure you don't hit the ball with a descending blow, which can

For optimum contact, play the ball one inch ahead of your sternum.

pinch the ball against the turf and influence the roll. It's also far enough back in your stance that the putterface will still be square to the target, assuming your stroke hasn't broken down.

You might wonder why the sternum is used as the initial point of reference for ball position, and not the feet. That would be simpler, wouldn't it, considering that they're so much closer to the ball? Yes, but the feet aren't always reliable. Consider this: If you position the ball just ahead of center relative to your feet, it will also be just ahead of the center of your sternum—if your weight is evenly distributed between both feet. But if you favor the front leg in your stance (Greg Norman and Nick Faldo do it), your torso shifts forward with your weight, so that same ball position—just ahead of center in your stance—will actually be *behind* the center of your sternum. You'll make contact before the putterhead reaches the bottom of its arc and trap the ball against the green. On the other hand, if you use your sternum as the reference point, you can be sure the ball position is correct every time.

A Word on Aim

All these specifics about the setup are actually only half of what you need to hit the ball the way you want. Aim is the other factor. Good aim is about setting the putterface square to the target; a good setup aligns the body relative to the putterface. Since aim is closely associated with the routine of actually executing a putt on the course, it will be discussed in the next chapter, "The Stroke."

6

Putting: The Stroke

Why does putting have to be so complicated? It's just a short little stroke made with a short little club. It's easy—certainly easier than hitting a full shot with, say, a 3-iron. Right?

Well, kind of. It's easier to make solid contact on a putt than it is on a long-iron shot, but in other ways, a putt is much more demanding. First of all, there's far less margin for error. If you hit a 3-iron from 190 yards to a green that's 20 yards wide, you can have varying degrees of success. Hitting the ball next to the pin is great, but just getting it on the green is pretty good, too. For that matter, missing the green but leaving yourself an easy chip shot isn't so bad, either—you still have a good chance at par. You can miss your target by 10 yards—that's 30 feet—and still feel good about yourself.

With putting, the target is only 4¼ inches wide, and there's only one way to be successful: by making the ball go in the hole. Missing is failure, whether it's by an inch or a foot, unless you're a long way from the hole and just trying to get down in two. But from inside 15 feet, there are only misses—which are no fun—and bad misses, when you leave yourself in position where you might miss again.

And what about distance control? You know approximately how far that 3-iron is going to go if you hit it well. So you only use it when you're the appropriate distance from the green; if you're closer, you take less club and make virtually the same swing. Distance control, for the most part, is out of your hands: The loft of the club and length of the shaft largely determine how far the ball will go. But on the green, the putter is the only club you use, regardless of distance. You determine how far the ball will roll based on how much effort you put into the stroke; it's all on you. So it may not be a physically challenging move, but the putting stroke demands a better sense for direction and distance than any other shot in golf.

A more familiar way to describe direction and distance on the green is by using the words "line" and "speed." To make an effective stroke for any given putt, you need to know what the line of the putt is (the path the ball will take to the hole) and have a sense for the speed (how hard to hit the ball so that it reaches the hole). These factors are fairly simple on a short, straight putt, but if the green is sloped between the ball and the hole, they're dependent on each other: You can't know the right line of a putt unless you have a feel for the speed; and the proper speed varies based on what line you want the ball to take. In that case, understanding line and speed is a process in itself, something that will be explored at length in Chapter Three. First, you have to be able to hit the ball straight. And that begins with proper alignment.

Aim and Alignment

Think in terms of a straight, 10-foot putt. As with full shots, it's easiest to aim the putterface to the hole first, then align your body perpendicular to the putterface. To begin the process, the putterface should be square—at a right angle to the line of the putt. Most putters have a little horizontal line etched into the top of the head designed to help you make sure the face is square. Once the face is square, align your body accordingly, starting with your feet. In a square setup, the lines of your feet,

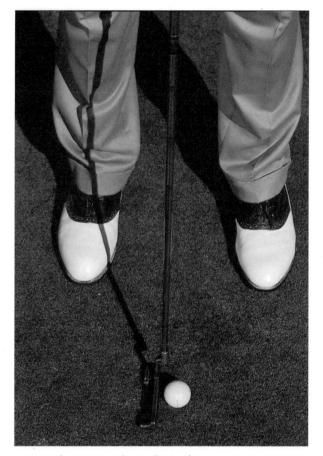

Square the putterface first, then set your stance
perpendicular to the face.

knees, hips, and shoulders are parallel to the line of
the putt, or perpendicular to the putterface. So,
with square aim and alignment and a straight-back,
straight-through stroke that returns the putterface
to the same square position at impact, the ball will
roll perfectly straight.

Aligning yourself for putts that break (curve to the right or left because of undulations in the green) is only slightly different. Instead of aiming the putterface at the hole, square it to the line on which the ball should start. That is, if the putt breaks six inches from right to left, aim the putterface six inches right of the hole, then align your body square to the putterface. From there, make the same straight-back, straight-through stroke you would for a straight putt. It's really that simple.

Spot Putting

Aiming the putterface is easy when the hole is three feet away, but what if it's 20 feet? It's much tougher to be precise and, therefore, feel confident that you're aiming the putter and yourself in the right direction. Wouldn't it be a shame to make a perfect stroke and miss the putt because your putterface and body were aligned just a fraction off-line?

Try spot putting instead. Crouch behind the ball and picture in your mind the line it will take to the hole. Then, choose a spot—an old ball mark or discolored patch of grass—about three feet in front of the ball and on that imaginary line. Instead of aim-

For accurate aim, line up to a spot a few feet in front of the ball.

ing the putterface at the hole, aim it to the spot you've chosen, three feet away. It's much easier to be sure of yourself with such a close target. Then, align your body perpendicular to the putterface and make your stroke. If you've read the putt correctly, the ball will roll over the spot and continue on into the hole.

The Three Elements of a Perfect Putt

To hit a perfect, on-line putt, three things have to happen at impact: The path of the putterhead has to be straight along the target line; the putterface has to be square to the target; and contact has to be made on the sweet spot of the putterface. To tell the truth, you can hit the ball on-line without perfect path, face angle, or contact, but it's a much easier game without trying to offset mistakes.

Two things occur if you strike a putt when your path is not straight along the target line. Assuming the face is still square to the target, sidespin is imparted to the ball, just like in the full swing. If the path goes from in to out, the ball will spin slightly from right to left as it rolls, encouraging the ball to go left and slowing it down. When the path is out to in, the ball spins from left to right, and tends to drift weakly to the right.

The other effect a faulty path has on a putt is starting direction. If the path goes to the left, the ball will typically start left. If the path is right, the ball will usually start right—even if the face remains square to the target line. That said, a faulty path probably gets too much credit for most missed putts. Since it's easy to see when your path is off, many players naturally assume that it's the main reason why the ball went off-line. But according to Dave Pelz, *GOLF Magazine*'s Technical and Short Game Consultant, there's a more likely culprit: face angle. A former scientist at NASA, Pelz has conducted exhaustive research on the physics of putting, and one of the many things he has discovered is that only 20 percent of a golfer's error in path is actually transmitted to the golf ball. Translated, that means if the putterhead is moving out to in, five degrees to the left of the target line, the ball will roll only one degree left of the target line, assuming the face is square to the target. That's about two inches on a 20-foot putt. So, a faulty path, while easy to see, has less effect on the ball's direction than you might imagine.

An error in face angle, on the other hand, is difficult to see—especially in somebody else's stroke—but Pelz's research shows that 90 percent of a golfer's error in face angle is transmitted to the golf ball. That means if the face is 10 degrees closed at impact, the ball will go 9 degrees left of the target line—and miss the hole by almost two feet on a 20-foot putt. So, when your putts miss the hole significantly to the right or left, your path may be off, but your face angle almost definitely is.

BEST TIP: Hit the Tee

Want to check your face angle at impact? Stick a tee in the end of a grip and lay the club on the green. Pretend the shaft is your target line. Set up to the tee and make your normal stroke: If the face is square, you'll tap the tee solidly; if it's open or closed, you'll knock the club off-line.

—Martin Hall, *GOLF Magazine* Master Teaching Professional

How about the third factor: solid contact? How important is that? First, you should understand what happens when you make contact off the sweet spot. If, for example, you make contact toward the toe of the putter, the heel kicks forward, the face twists open, and less energy is imparted to the ball.

BEST TIP: Band-Aid Cure

Wrap two Band-Aids around the face of the putter so the pads form a half-inch frame of the sweet spot. If you make contact in the middle of the face, the putt will come off as usual. But if you make contact off center, the ball will hit one of the pads and roll about half as far. As solid contact becomes easier, move the Band-Aids closer together.

—Darrell Kestner, *GOLF Magazine*
Top 100 Teacher

Chances are, the putt will finish farther right and shorter than you were expecting. Exactly how much depends on how the putter you're using is constructed, but Pelz found that, on average, an eight-foot putt hit a quarter inch toward the toe will miss the hole 95 percent of the time. Clearly, the farther you get from the hole, the worse the odds get. The putting stroke may be a small motion, but don't take solid contact for granted; it's too important to ignore.

Common Faults

Straight stroke, square face, solid contact—simple, right? Think about it for a second: It's not like you're trying to make a full shoulder turn and drive the legs and clear the hips and finish in balance. It's a simple, pendulum-like motion controlled by the arms and shoulders. Weather and course conditions play a part, but mostly, if you're missing putts it's because you're making mistakes—adding flaws to a simple activity. The physical challenge of putting is less about achieving kinesthetic brilliance than it is avoiding mistakes.